Letters

to

Ella Lee Goode

A COLLECTION
OF
TURN-OF-THE-CENTURY CORRESPONDENCE
FROM
LOUDOUN COUNTY, VIRGINIA

1896–1900

Edited and Compiled by

Meridee Orndoff Mucciarone

HERITAGE BOOKS
2015

HERITAGE BOOKS

AN IMPRINT OF HERITAGE BOOKS, INC.

Books, CDs, and more—Worldwide

For our listing of thousands of titles see our website
at
www.HeritageBooks.com

Published 2015 by
HERITAGE BOOKS, INC.
Publishing Division
5810 Ruatan Street
Berwyn Heights, Md. 20740

International Standard Book Numbers
Paperbound: 978-1-58549-869-7
Clothbound: 978-0-7884-9240-2

In memory of my mother
Margaret Kathryn Albaugh Orndoff
Margaret's daughter
Ella Lee's granddaughter

✤ Contents

Introduction

Samuel Perry Goode died in 1892 at the age of 41, days after the birth of his ninth child. He was buried in Ketoctin Cemetery in Loudoun County. His family endured many hardships after his death as they tried to make ends meet on their farm near Purcellville, Virginia.

During the years from 1896 through 1900, Ella Lee, the eldest child of Sam and Margaret Goode, was working as a seamstress in Washington, D.C. She and her cousin Nettie Simpson worked downtown from the fall months until the end of spring, either renting a room or staying with the family they were working for at the time. Relatives and friends would come and go, visiting or looking for work themselves. Others would write of the news of home. Ella saved many of the letters written to her from family and friends during this time, most of them from Loudoun County, Virginia. Sometimes she sent stamps to her mother so that she could send her the news. These letters portray the day-to-day life of the time in a rural area, complete with road conditions, illnesses, gossip, church activities, births, deaths, marriages, and weather reports.

The first letters are mostly from family members. Samuel Goode was originally from St. Mary's County in Maryland and some of the letters are from the Goode family relatives that still lived there. Colorful letters came from Ella's immediate family in Purcellville, Virginia. Another group of correspondence came from the branch of the family in Northern Virginia.

Samuel Goode's brother Ed lived in Aldie, Virginia, with his wife and young children. Ed's sister-in-law, Maude Ellison, lived with them and was a good friend of Ella's. From the letters it is surmised that Maude introduced Ella Lee to John Bodmer of Aldie. At least half of the letters are written by John Bodmer and chronicle their growing romance. He and Ella were married soon after the letters stop.

The letters are supplemented by as many old photos and relevant material as could be found. Family trees are presented in the back of the book, along with accounts of later times. Finally, an index of names and places is included for anyone searching for information about these families or ancestors from Loudoun County.

Acknowledgments

Much of the credit for the creation of this book goes to the late Elfrida Martin, my mother's best friend. Elfrida gathered the beginnings of the included family tree information and her records together with the found letters set in motion the idea for this book. I consider myself most fortunate that she included my family as part of her own.

My search for facts to accompany the letters led me to the Balch Library in Leesburg, Virginia. The staff there was very helpful and the library is a wonderful resource. I would also like to thank my uncle Paul Albaugh for his assistance with family history and photos.

Finally, I would like to acknowledge my sisters Lorena Orndoff and Crystel Kurtzberg who helped with the preparation of the manuscript, and my husband Kirk and my sons Anthony and Steven for their encouragement.

❧ 1896–1898

Dynard, Md.
April 14, 1896

Dear friend,

I received your letter quite a long time ago but was in too much trouble to answer it. I suppose you heard about little Edwin being dead. Oh Lee, it almost broke my heart to part from him but the Lord's will must be done and now he is a bright little angel in heaven and I must try to forget him. But it will be many a day before I will forget that dear little boy. Lee, I have another baby and it is a boy also. He was born on Good Friday. Just two weeks after little Edwin died. But I don't think I will ever care for any more babies. I think he is very much like Mamie. I have never kissed him yet. You must write me word what to name him.

Well I hope this may find you well. They are all well but me and you can't expect me well yet and the baby not two weeks old until Friday. But I have been upstairs once and in the dining room often. I got dinner today. I want to go out next week if it keeps good weather. Webster is planting corn today. It is very warm. I would like to be out in the garden to work. So much to do and I can't do any.

Well I suppose you have some chickens by this time. I have got 10 little bits of dried up things. I don't expect to have any soon.

Lee, the wind has not blown me in the river yet but you know I have been in the house most all the time so it don't get a shoe. It has been right windy all through lent but I am in hopes we are going to have some good weather. Lee, I hope you may come down this summer and stay a while with me as you was so mean last winter you would not stay none with me. Don't let this make you mad now because you might not come at all next time. If you was down now you could get plenty of oysters. Mrs. Good and your Uncle Jim was up to see Rose last Monday and she knew I was sick but she never came to see me and she stayed up there all day. But I don't believe anybody cares for me. It don't seem so to me. She came up there one day before I moved and she never came in my room at all. I don't know what I have done to her but she doesn't seem to like me. But I won't cry if she never comes. It is all right to me.

Georgy stays with us now. Cecie was up yesterday evening. She said her mother was little better. You know she has not been well since you left down here.

Well I will bring my letter to a close. Goodbye, write soon and please excuse bad writing and all my mistakes for they are plenty of them in this letter but I guess you can make them out some how. My hands are so trembly I can't half write. I hope to hear from you soon. From your old friend

Emma G.

TO: *Miss Ella L. Good and Escort, West End, Va.*

1897

Your presence is requested at a Public Debate
of the Law School Debating Society of
Columbian University ❧ ❧ ❧

At University Hall,
Saturday, November 20, 1897
at 8 o'clock p. m.

Ralph H. Riddleberger, of Va., President.
Howard S. Lewis, of Kans., Chairman Ex. Com.

Subject: Resolved, That the Hawiian Islands should be annexed
to the United States.

Affirmative:

I. O. H. Alward, N. J.   F. P. Hopgood, N. C.   F. N. Church, N. J.

Negative:

J. W. Crooks, Ill.   E. E. Denison, Ill.   J. B. Aird, Ala.

Judges:

Judge W. A. Maury.   Hon. C. W. Needham.   Prof. L. D. Lodge.

BLACK HEARTED.

You false and empty-hearted flirt,
  Your heart's as wicked as your mind;
'Tis filled with venom, pride, and hate,
  Against the rest of human kind.
Love never touched your flinty heart,
  Its pains and pleasures all unknown;
While Envy like a serpent's sting,
  In you a passion fierce has grown.

REJECTED.

'Tis very hard lines thus to love and be smitten—
To offer your hand and then get the mitten;
That very fair rose will no doubt be rejected and blue
For snubbing so sweet a gallant as you.
Keep a stiff upper lip though she turns up her nose,
There's men quite as ugly have stood in your clothes.

Falls Church
Jan 19th, 1898

My dear Ella,

Your letter, rec'd some time ago, will answer. Well I have had company for two weeks, my Aunt Susie Monroe, her son and daughter. They live at Unison Va, will go home Friday.

Well Ella, Maurice has joined the Marine Band. Had his suit on Sat. in Falls Church, looks out of sight. Poor Charlie R. is very sick, come down and nurse him. I have been on the go all the time just sporting around. Geo was up Sunday and was as nice as you please. Ella, he is a peach. Frank still comes up. He and I do not speak. Fell out Sunday night about smoking in the parlor. Geo put me up to it but what do I care. Ella, I do not expect to come up very soon in your part of the country. Berkley is going to drive up the 1st of Feb. for a week and I am going with him to Unison to see Tom. I have not laid eyes on Joe Allen since the night he was in the (Cold Storage) and I do not care if I never do. Joe Hill has been up in New York for his health and is now in the city again.

I was down at Mrs. Taylor's tonight. All are well. Saw Mr. Ives. He is well and as sweet as ever. Say Ella, Mrs. Mankins is going to have a baby. What do you think of that? Wouldn't that be nice if you were there to take care of her now? John and Edith were down during the holiday. She is growing. Minnie has set on Norman—goes with Everett Johnson now. Ella, Bertha Capner is still lieing. Mag is working against me and Geo. Don't know how things will end. Elmer and Howard are getting along nice. I make these people eat in the kitchen around the stove to one side of the room and table the other side.

I will close, hope you will not be so long writing. No news in this town. The Good Templars gave Mr. Hawxhuysh a surprise party last Friday night. I did not go but Mag and Minnie did. The protracted meetings are going on at the Presbyterian Church. Say, Coon Lowe gave me a nice pocket book for Xmas present but I hate him. He still follows me. Will Sprankle and Sarah Man are married. Sharp Crossman and Miss Smith married last week. I will be next. We have a dull time now. Lodge is not worth going to. Write soon. How is Web? Who is his girl? Hastily

Lelia

Alexandria Va.
Feb. 15, 1898

Dear Friend,

According to promise I will write and let you know how I am getting along. I am well and having a lovely time. I went to church twice
on Sunday to hear Mr. Butler preach. I like him very much but of
course not so well as I do Mr. Lake. I am invited to an entertainment
tonight for the benefit of the church but I guess I will not go for it is
raining very hard. A gentleman wanted me to go to the opera Saturday night but I told him no for I promised someone before I left
home I would not go and you know *I never break a promise.* I do think
there are some of the ugliest men down here I ever saw, not handsome like the Loudoun men. I want to go to Washington the last of
this week, and I will go to see Johnie (is that his name) Welby and
one of my old beaus.

I have not had a good night sleep since I have been here. The
Salvation Army preaches on the corner every night and they seem to
draw great crowds. Tell Blanche Bertha sends her love and says she is
still looking for a letter from her. I suppose you got a valentine. I
never saw as many as there are down here, but I did not get any. Tell
Blanche she must be sure and take good care of Sam until I come
home. Please excuse my bad letter for the children are keeping so
much racket I can hardly think. I have not heard from home yet but
I want to write again tonight to some of them. Give my love to Miss
Mary or in fact all my friends. Write soon and a long letter too.

Aurie B. L.

Direct your letter to 1117 22nd St., Washington D.C.

March 7, 1898
Falls Church

Dear Ella,

I have not heard from you in so long I thought I would send you a few lines this morning. I was out to an entertainment Friday night, when I was coming out and right in the biggest crowd I heard some-one say "Hello Mother." I knew that meant me so I began to look around and there was my boy Maurice. I could not say much to him in the crowd but I promised I would send you his address and ask you to write to him. Ella, he thinks much of you, he said he would write you but you had not answered it and he did not like to write again until you did. Ella, he is liable to be sent out to Spanish waters any how and it would be a comfort to him to hear from you. His address is Maurice Buroes, Washington, DC.

Now Ella do write to him right away won't you. I must close with love to all. I am your ever loving friend

Mrs. Mabon

Falls Church, Va.
Mar. 7, 1898

My dear Ella:

Will write you a few lines. Guess you have forgotten us as I wrote you a letter about two months ago and you have never answered. But I guess Clarence takes all your spare time. Saw Maurice Friday and he is a bird in his uniform. Well Ella, I am going to Cuba to fight—are you? I hear that Mrs. Mabon wrote to you to come and help her again. Is it so? Ella, I have just had a lively time lately. Edith has been down. She is expecting the 28th of this month. You know that is the next thing after you marry is to get a kid. What is the matter you don't write? Papa still goes with Em. She has had all her teeth pulled out. Frank still holds forth, was up last night, is coming again tomorrow night. I am sec. in Lodge. We have some hot times at Lodge now. Lelia and Mr. Birch are cutting quite a figure.

Old Mrs. Lynch fell and broke her arm last week. She is very bad off. She is at Mrs. Mankin's. You know Mrs. Mankin is strictly in it— she is expecting this month some time. Mrs. Lynch came to wait on her and fell and broke her arm.

Looking for Guy Luttrell's death at any time.

I tell you Falls Church is a fine place. Conference meets here Wednesday. You come down and attend. We expect two preachers and two ladies. Lelia is staying all night with Mrs. Swift. Minnie has a blue suit, she says come down tomorrow and make it for her. I will not write much this time. See if you are going to answer this one. What are you doing? Write me all the news. How are you and Clarence getting along? How is Arthur? Remember me to him. Give my love to all your folks and save a share for yourself. I will close.

Good night, write soon, come down sooner

Lovingly,
Maggie

TO: *Miss Ella L. Goode, 815 22nd St., N.W., Washington DC*

Purcellville Va.
Mar 22, 1898

Dear Lee,

Your card just received this eve, I send your Queen of Fashion today. I send the March Number. You did not say which so I thought that was the latest one. If it is torn a little, don't hurt it I don't think. Laura told me a Sunday when I was down there that it was all right. I told her you had written to me to send your book, that you thought she would think you were going to keep her money. She said she did not think any such thing. Said you told her she would get a pattern free and said you could pick out one that you thought would suit for Norah as she expected you would come down before you left and you did not. It is all right, she says anyway.

Well this leaves us as well as ever as the colds are about well, all except mother. I don't reckon she will ever be any better as she has been like this so long with such a cough, too weak too. Kate and the

Children of Peregrine Goode and Ellen Cartwright (m. 1/25/1837)

1. Thomas William   b. 2/11/1841; m. Elisabeth Sine
2. Lucinda A.   b. 9/1844; m. Kingsley Davis
3. James Henry   b. 2/9/1846; m. 1. Ellen Turner
                                                       2. Rebecca H. Copsey
4. Samuel Perry   b. 9/8/1850; d. 8/5/92
                                                m. Margaret Clara Settle 1/22/1873
5. John B.   b. 10/17/1857; m. Theresa Grubb
6. Mary Jane   d. died young, unmarried
7. Edward Benjamin   b. 12/17/61; d. 1934; m. Eliza Ellison

Records from family Bible — Source Annie Goode Ish as listed in *Notes on Goode Family History* by Sister Teresa Clare.

babes are tolerable well. Oscar is so bad she can't have a bit of pleasure, as soon as she gets the baby put down then he cries for her to hold him. Won't let any one else hold him and sometimes he cries for her to take him while she has the baby. Then she has to hold both.

I got a few lines from John Goode today—wrote to me to send for the horse he was to let me have to plow. Said they were all well. That is about all he wrote. They are all well at Purcellville. The little pigs are doing very nice, sweet and nice. The little chicks are doing real nice but today something hurt one and it died, but the 9 are looking all right. Now the turkeys are laying. I have 4 eggs. One of them broke an egg yesterday as soon as she laid it. Was her first egg. I got my rooster from Laura yesterday and have 3 hens setting and three will set tomorrow. Perry is down to Ed's, went yesterday. It is too wet to plow so he has not come home yet. Clarence S. is here tonight. He stayed last night too. Tell Rosa I will write to her as soon as I can get 2c more. I have to beg this or borrow. Tell her Stanley is home now. I heard W. S. has lost his position but is about to get another place. I guess has by this time.

Mary Cooper was asking about you the other day. Said if she had known you were home she would of come over to see you. Said she surely did like that girl, she was so nice. Sam Hough was at Ed's Sunday, him and Harry, and they surely did carry on, them and Ed. I just thought while Kate was here I would go down there and spend the day. I don't know when I enjoyed myself as well. I went horseback too.

Mrs. Lang has moved. Yes, Miss Sallie went home to get ready to move so they moved the 15th but Mrs. L and Kate both were not able to go. They had been poorly I suppose with colds but they thought they would be able to move. But when they were moving they had to be taken over to Mr. Jenkins their neighbor so I have not heard where they have ever been able to go yet or not. Perry went up there and took Miss Sallie and Doll and Jessie Gayner. She went with them to help. Miss Sallie sent for me to come up and help them a little the day before they moved and to stay all night but I sent her word I could not possibly do it for the children had such colds and Grandma too, that I had to doctor them all night. So now they are city folks in Hamilton. Annie More told me Sunday that Bessie W and Garland was to be married in April and was coming up to Reids to have a dinner. I don't know whether to believe it or not. Or has him and Verge married? What is Verge doing? Has she work? I am glad you found her. I guess it was a very happy meeting. Give my love to her. I think Rosa ought not to put up on Cousin B so long, or has she found anything to do yet?

Where is Mr. Gould? You never say anything about him. Who was the young man that called on you? You say I don't know him. Or was it Hemsted Hunter. He seemed to be pleased very much when I told him about the pants. I have not seen Mr. Beans since I got your letter. I don't hear him say any more about marrying so you ought to took him before you went away. I am afraid he won't be in the notion very soon again. I think he just had a spell on him when you were here. He came by here from Eubanks, him and Harry once, since you went and he said he thought he had better make some arrangements for he was nearly dead. Said he did not think he could stay here very long but he was getting all right. Then I have not seen him since I patched him one pair pants.

Well I don't think I know of anything else to write now. Write when you can have time. Give my love to Nettie and tell her not to try to kick too high if she can she might have an accident. All send their love to you, say they want to see Lee. Lovingly

Ma
(Margaret Clara Settle Goode)

You could drop me a card if you can't write a letter and let me know if the Queen of Fashion is all right. If this is not right I will send the Feb. No.

Ella's mother, Margaret Clara Settle Goode

March the 29, 1898
Dynard PO

Dear Old Friend,

As I have not heard from you for so long a time I thought I would write you a few lines to let you know I am still living after a long spell of sickness. I have been sick ever since we moved up here. Not been able to do anything hardly but thanks to the good Lord I am out again after a hard time. Lee, I suppose you heard I had another girl. I tell you I liked to died. I had to have the doctor. I guess Rosey thought I was in a bad way when she and Cecie came up here. Lee, why was it you never answered my last letter? I looked so long for an answer from you till I gave up and said that I know Lee is not going to write any more to me. But I thought—I would like to hear from you once more as I never hear from you. I did hear Bruce say where you were and what you was doing.

What is the matter with Georgy? Has he forgotten you or have you forsaken him? I heard you and him do not write any more. I have not seen Georgy since last November when he was living with us. He was always down to see Marion but he never comes up here. But if he doesn't want to come I don't want to see him. Duglas is the best friend Webster has. I see him often. Marion has been up once since we moved. I have not seen Rose since last September but I have been sick all the time, not able to go from home. I have not been from home since Christmas only down to Cora's. I wanted to go to church Saturday to have the baby christened but I don't think I will be able to go fore I am a long ways from being well. I am going to give the baby the name Ella Francies and call her Ella and name her after you. Lee, you must come down to see me this summer. I certainly would be glad to see you. So would Cora for she seems to think a lot of you. I will take you around this time if Georgy will not but I guess if you was to come down to my house he would break his neck getting up here. I have plenty of room if my house is small.

Webster bought land from his Father and we expect to build a house next year if nothing happens. Webster and his Father are getting along all right. They have been done plowing some time. We have been gardening sometime. My peas and onions are up and looking pretty and I have a few chickens. Compton and Mamie say they would like to see you. Little Elmer has not been very well this last week. Sunday is his birthday. He will be two years old.

Lee I have a lot more to tell you but I am afraid my letter is getting too long. You must excuse this bad writing and all my mistakes for you know I do the very best I can. I would have written to you before but did not know your address until Sunday. Bruce gave me your address. They all join me in love to you. Well I will say good day. Write soon as I would be very glad to hear from you. From your true friend,

Emma Good

TO: *Miss Ella L. Goode, 815 22nd St., N.W., Washington, D.C./ 11 School St.*

LIST OF GOODS WANTED OF
THE TABB & JENKINS HARDWARE COMPANY.

Purcellville, Va.
April 3, 1898

I will try to answer your letter at last as you sent me a stamp. I will use it for you also. Rosa sent me one and so I have written to her tonight. You say you want me to write a long letter and tell you all the news. I don't know much news to tell. I never go anywhere and so I never hear anything. There seems to be a good bit of war talk. It almost scares me. Now does it scare you? I think you better come home before they get to work at it. I hope there will be none.

Well this leaves all well. As usual Grandma was not well but she went home with Kate last Wednesday. Oscar said he wanted Aunt Lee, boy he cried to come back when he got home. He said going along he was going home but he was coming back again. Eva is getting plumper every day. Ed and Laura went up to Jim's yesterday and took Kings and Cinda. Perry was to keep house. He was up here this morning and went to church, him and Wade, but soon as they came back from church they went back to Ed's. Perry has hired to Ed by the month so now I have no one to do a thing. Have to hire it done or do it myself. That is a poor shame ain't it. Mr. Bean and Harry was up last Monday and got up stumps—got up 132. Perry was here to help. Perry went over to John Goode's and got a cold so I don't know when we can work it much or not. Sent off Lizzie's calf last Monday. Got $5.91 for it. Old Lizzie is the worst cow to milk. Have to pen her up. She kicks like a horse. She gives about 1 gal. I think it is just as good as Daisy's too, looks rich. Mr. Bean sent his love to you. The old sow won't drink hardly any slop. I give her nice milk, but the old fool don't like it. She won't drink as much as I can. She eats corn all right but I would rather for her to drink slop to make her give milk for the pigs. We don't get many eggs now. I have 8 hens on hen eggs and 3 on duck eggs. I have about 18 turkey eggs.

Well by the way, Miss Lizzie Hughes is started her meeting in Purcellville. Sam has gone out tonight and took Miss Sue Lanham and I guess his horse will be gone. Claud also went. He walked. Clarence is here. He stays with us every night since Perry has been gone. I guess he likes to though. Rather stay here than to go to church. The converts out here since she commenced and that was Thursday night was John Benedum, Henry France, John Smith, Turner Brother and another old man. Web Lang and Clint Benedum joined at Silcott Springs or Lincoln I don't know which. But was converted at Silcott Springs. There was over 40 converted at Silcott Springs. I don't know how long she will carry it on at Purcellville. Mollie Bean has a new machine just like the one I had, I guess it is the same one, she got it from Atley. I think ought to give me his don't you?

Well I dreamed about you and J. Gould last night. I dreamed he tried to get your letter from me and you told me to hold fast to it. What are you and him doing? That Harry and Clarence D. went over to John Goode's Thursday and stayed till Saturday on a visit. Clarence said there is Lee's trunk. He had the key but he did not get in it. I have not made any garden yet—it is too cold out today. Ice was here today at the pump, I know all the fruit is killed.

Well I can't think of anything else for I am so sleepy. No, mother has not been to see Andie any more. Old Mr. Thorp has moved in with Eva. He has been living at Loyds. I don't know anything about him or who he is. Well I guess I will close for I can't think of any more tonight. Give my love to Nettie, tell her I love her. Write soon.

I forgot to tell you Clarence Davis said hurry up and come home. You had the headache and he had the bellyache so you and him ought to be together. So hurry. He was like a wild cat—no sense in him. Well good night, with love, from your loving mother

Ma

Lee, I wrote to Burr W' and Rosa did not tell me where it was, N.E. or S.E. or which way. I am afraid it is not right and after I put the stamp on I did not want to loose it so I put it in your letter. I thought perhaps you will know. I would have put it in Rosa's letter but I had the stamp on hers and had not put it on yours so I will put it in your letter. If not too much trouble some time when you get a chance will you please send it to him if you can. Rosa never said where she went to see him since he came back so I thought I would write to him myself and see what he says. No use to be contrary to him for he won't pay no way if he will at all. I will wait a little longer.

Ma

TO: *Miss Ella Goode, 815 22nd St., N.W., Washington, D.C.*

Lincoln, Va.
Apr 12th, 1898

My dear Ella,

I was so glad to get your letter. I feel like giving you a little lecture for not writing to me sooner; and then you didn't come to see me while you were home. I looked for you and can assure you that you would have been welcomed. I wish it had been so I could have gone to see you while you were home, but please excuse me this time, as I had no way to come. Oh, well! I guess you did not give me many thoughts about that time, as I heard you were busily engaged in making shirts for that old bachelor friend of yours. Did they fit "all right"?

So Mr. Trundle bed has gone to Spanish waters and you are so sad. Indeed the threatening war is quite enough to make us all feel uneasy. I sincerely hope Mr. T. will not be killed or wounded, and will in a short time return to his country and to you. Don't let J. Gould go. I might cry. Has he been to call on you yet?

I am so sorry you were not in Washington Xmas. I am quite sure I could have found your boarding place. I wish I was there now. It is so very, very quiet here. I think if the girls keep on leaving Loudoun we'll have to import a few. Sallie Downs has gone to Halifax Co. Va. Bessie is in Washington. Marcie Birdsall is in Mecklenburg, Va. Sallie and Marcie have gone as milliners. You see the girls are all leaving. I guess I will have to follow the fashion and go somewhere too. Don't you want me to come down and keep you company while you sew? Perhaps I can go out to Langley occasionally. I am not so sure that I like you to be so near Langley. Don't you think too much of John B. for I think a great deal of him myself. We might scratch each others eyes out if we both get to liking him too well.

And you haven't forgotten how to make chocolate cake yet. Be sure to not eat it all, save a little piece and send it to Loudoun. I'll see that he gets it all right. Mr. C— has been sick for three weeks, but I guess not too sick to eat chocolate cake. He is missed very much in the Sunday School.

Dr. A. L. Jones will this evening at six o'clock lead to the altar Miss Lucy E. Churchill. They are to be married in Frostburg Md., at the residence of Hon. J. B. Oden, brother-in-law of Miss C—. I suppose it will be quite a fine affair. Two hundred and seventy-five invitations have been sent. Indeed, I feel as if I would like to be present, but that will be impossible, it is so far away, about 200 miles from Front Royal. I had a letter from Arch this morning. He said he did not feel one bit nervous. They expect to go to Baltimore for a few days and then return to Front Royal. Will not come home until later.

Several families in this neighborhood have moved this spring. We have Mr. C. Downs for a neighbor. He is farming Mr. Curl's property. Mrs. Emily Janney has moved back to her old home. Mr. S. Bolyn moved into the house vacated by Mrs. Janney. Mrs. Dowdell has gone to Lincoln to the Janney house. Mr. Lemon has moved to Mr. Bolyn's house. Old Mr. Fenton has purchased Jonathan Silcott's house in Lincoln and will move there before long.

Miss Mary L. Hughes is conducting a series of meetings at Purcellville. I heard today that Clint and Walter Benedum have been converted. I hope that much good may be done. Is Rosa in Washington yet? I have not seen Eddie for a long time. He expected to pay us a visit of a few days about a month ago, but on account of the weather did not come.

Don't forget to give my very best love to Nettie and tell her I thought of her while in Washington, but did not know where to find her. I think I have written you all the news I know of and I expect you are tired of reading long before you get to the last sheet so I will not write any more.

You must write to me again and tell me all about yourself. Lucie is "poorly" and doesn't feel like saying anything. She doesn't eat much. Mamma says tell you that she is well, and can still eat chocolate cake.

> Very truly your friend,
> Orra Jones

TO: *Miss Ella L. Goode, 11 School St., Washington, D.C.*

> Purcellville, Va.
> April 17, 1898

Dear Lee,

I will write to you at last. I would of written sooner but every night I have to patch and in day I have to work out doors. So this is Sunday night, and I will try to write a little. I have written Rosa a few lines too. This leaves us all well. Hope this will find you quite well. No use to be too scared about the war. I hope it won't be much but I don't see any papers so I don't know what is going on. We hear different news so I don't know what to believe. Old Lillie is still living. I heard Mr. Brown is going to sell her. He is selling off all his old cows. Mrs. Seaton's daughter lives there, Ella Smith, and they said so don't dream of her and cry no more.

Well Lee, I don't know how to get your trunk to you. If I had known I might of sent it today by Garland and Bessie Wiley but did not know they were up until they were ready to start back. Mother just came back from Purcellville and she said they went back this evening. I don't know when Arthur will go. I will see him and ask him. Mother said he told Bessie that he was coming down when he made some money. They have commenced work on Thursday evening last.

Ma'Mam's Marble Cake

INGREDIENTS

Bowl 1	Bowl 2 (white)	Bowl 3 (spice)
4 egg whites	2 cups unbleached flour	2 cups unbleached flour
	1 cup sugar	1 cup (packed) brown
	2 tsp baking powder	sugar
	1/2 tsp salt	1 tsp baking soda
	1/2 cup butter (softened)	1/2 tsp salt
	2/3 cup milk	2 tsp cinnamon
	1 or 2 tsp vanilla	2 tsp nutmeg
		1/2 tsp cloves
		1/2 cup butter
		(softened)
		2/3 cup buttermilk
		4 egg yolks
		1/2 cup molasses

DIRECTIONS *(with editorial comments)*

This is a 3 bowl recipe, and if you go in the order: egg whites, white mix, spice mix, then you don't need to wash the beaters in between bowls.

My family usually makes this as a bundt cake with what we call a sampler. The sampler is a small layer cake, which takes up the extra batter. If you bake the cake in an angel food pan you can try skipping the sampler. A normal bundt pan is usually a little too small.

Grease and flour the pans you intend to use. Take your time preheating the oven to 350, because it usually takes about 1/2 hour to get the cake in the oven.

I usually mix the dry ingredients in each of bowls 2 and 3, then add the wet ingredients to each, and put the egg whites in their own separate bowl. If you substitute margarine for butter, add about 1 tbsp of margarine to each bowl.

Beat the egg whites until stiff. You can add a pinch of salt and sugar to the egg whites if you want, but they'll work fine without that. Beat the white cake mix (bowl 2) for a few minutes, until creamy and fluffy. This batter is a little stiff, but it becomes more workable later when you fold in the egg whites. Beat the spice cake mix (bowl 3) for a few minutes, until fluffy. Fold the egg whites into the white cake batter.

Spoon the batter into the bundt pan to create a marble effect: pick either the white or spice batter, and spoon in three big dollops evenly spaced around the pan. Then top those dollops with batter from the other bowl. Keep alternating batters until you have the pan 1/2 to 2/3 full. Do the same with the sampler to use up the rest of the batter. Use a butter knife to swirl the batter so it has a marbled look. I usually start with the knife inserted near the outside of the pan and use the knife to draw a spiral in toward the middle. Be careful not to scrape the pan (bottom or sides), as that will make the cake stick to the pan.

Bake at 350° until done. This will depend entirely upon the pan(s) you use. A sampler usually takes 20 to 30 minutes and is done when it has pulled away from the sides of the pan, and springs back when touched. You can also use a toothpick to test it. It's done when you get a few loose crumbs on the toothpick (or a clean toothpick). A bundt cake usually takes about an hour. If it starts to brown too much on top, loosely cover it with tin foil.

The sampler can be turned out onto a plate or cooling rack to cool. The bundt cake needs to cool in the pan. It will most likely fall apart if you try to take it out of the pan when it's still hot. This cake generally becomes moister if it sits overnight (well covered/wrapped).

It goes well with whipped cream or ice cream.

Ella Lee's recipe for Marble Cake contributed by Lorena Orndoff

Cinda and Oscar was up here last week nearly the week. Kings came up after Cinda. Wanted her to salt their fish. He can't do it. I got my fish yesterday, a few, they are very nice too. Oscar said he wants Aunt Lee to get him a book. He always says that every time we ask him what to tell Aunt Lee he says book. He likes to stay up here, only when Clarence S. comes then he is scared and cries for someone to take him. I had company today, Nellie and Ethel and little Tommy. He sure is fat and cute. Clarence Davis, I have not seen him since he was here to go to John Goode's.

The colt does very well if there was anyone to work him. Clarence S has worked him a little and he does very well. Then Perry told me the other day he would come home and plow the lot when it would do Ed will let him off to. I have not sold the pigs yet—several have spoken for them but I don't know whether they will take them or not. They have grown right smart but the old sow is awful poor. I am soon going to take the pigs away from her. I have just put out 63 little chickens. Had only 12 besides them. I have some duck eggs hatching. I have not set any turkey eggs yet.

Lee don't say anything out of the way to Burr Wildman if you see him... until I see whether he will pay me. Then I don't care what you say but we will have to be quiet with him and see what he will do. I know he will do better if we are mild than he will if we talk rough so hold in a while if possible. I don't know any news. By the way, Sam Elmore has gone to church to Purcellville and taken Miss Lee. My house is gone. Would not turn his head towards the house. Clarence S. was here. He must have been afraid we would see him.

Good Mollie Beans has got her silk waist made in style. Lacy Hirst made it for her. She was inquiring about you. Asked when you were coming home. I told her I did not know. I reckon if there was war you would come soon.

Give my love to Nettie and Miss Eliza when you see her. I guess I will have to close. I can't think of anymore to write now and it is getting late so will say goodbye. Write soon, from your loving

Ma

Love to you and Nettie

P.S. Welby Seaton has gone back to the first place he went when he went to city—some Carr. I think a little out of city. It is funny what has become of J. Gould.

Lee, will you sell me the old sow? If so what will you take for her? The reason I want to buy, I would like to kill her next winter and keep a pig to raise from. I don't like her very much for a brood sow so if you will sell her I will buy, if not all right. I will pay you next fall if not before.

Ma

TO: *Miss Ella Goode, 11 School St., Mt. Pleasant, D.C.*

Baltimore
May 1, 1898

Dear Lee

I am on my way to Baltimore, will be there by the morning. We left home this morning. I intended to come to Washington last week but the weather was so bad and rainy I couldn't. The boat I intended to come up on didn't get home until Wednesday and it stormed the balance of the week so I changed my mind and came to Baltimore with Capt. Russell. I surely would of liked to come up to see you but I could make a trip that would be cheaper to me and of course I will have to go the way it is the cheapest in the future. I used to not mind it until I learned to know better. I left them all well except Rose. She is feeling quite badly.

What was the cause of Rosa going home? I surely think that it is the best place for her. Kids ought to be home with their mother. I have learned lots these days. More than I have to know. I suppose you and your Blacksmith are getting along all right. I guess they will soon have him down in Cuba blowing over the Spanyard. I suppose that is the reason you want to go. I wish there was someone that would follow me down there but it would be someone would have but a little brain.

Well Lee we have reached Baltimore. We got here about five o'clock this morning. We had it calm this morning. I am awful bad off. I have the toothache so bad I am most wild. My jaw is hurting so bad I can hardly open my mouth and I am sick other ways. I had bad luck when I came home. They all had gone up town except the cook and myself. I felt too bad to go and I had started this letter. I thought

I would finish it. We will be here until Friday morning. We have a little freight to land and we are going to take back a load of fertilizer. I expect to be home Sunday morning if nothing happens.

Well the United States has very strict orders. They don't allow any boats to pass Fort Carroll after sundown. One of the United States boats passed us this morning. Well I am going out in the morning to get some clothes. They are lots cheaper here than they are in Washington. Well I don't expect to come to Washington until some time in June. I have got a crab contract and I expect will have to go every three weeks after the money. The same man wants me part of May to clerk in store. I reckon I will.

You must excuse this short letter for I am feeling awful bad. I must stop and lie down. Well I must stop and bring my scribbling to a close. Hoping this will find you well. I will say goodbye with love from your cousin, and will be very glad to hear from you at anytime

Geo

TO: Miss Ella Lee Goode, #11 School St., Mt. Pleasant, D.C.

At Home (postmarked Falls Church)
May 4, 98

My dear Ella,

I know you will pardon me for not answering sooner but I lost your letter and did not know your number and just found it this a.m. Well we are having some lovely weather. Guess you are very sad over Maurice being so far away. Did Geo. come up last week? Who is your best beau now? How is that young lady that was out with you? We all like her very much. Ella, Elmer has traded his colt for another colt. See he believes in colts. His old girl Dorothy Searle spent last week with us. Howard said it only took Elmer from 11 o'clock until 3 to get his dinner and come to supper and stay all night.

Give my love to Miss Nettie. I am looking for Frank this eve. He said he saw you and Rosie that Sunday. Has Rosie gone home yet? Just to think I will be 22 yrs old next week. I will soon be a bachelor girl. Ella, come out and help enjoy our hammock. You know you are always welcome. I have not been to the city for a long time and do not know when I will be in. Don't wait for us. You come out when you can. Protracted meetings are going on at the Baptist Church. You come out and attend them. I went to Lodge last night. Measles and Scarlet Fever all in this town. I am glad I have had the measles. I went to the Good Fellows banquet last Thursday night. Had a large time. I danced two sets.

Mr. Spear, Mrs. Burches father, died this a.m. I do not know any more news to tell you. Write soon and come out to see us. Your loving friend

Maggie

P.S. Ella, Lelia says her Grandpa is dead, you know, George's Grandpa. *See*.

TO: Miss Ella L. Goode, #11 School Street, Mt. Pleasant, D.C.

Purcellville, Va.
May 6, 1898

Dear Lee,

I will try to write you a few lines tonight. It is raining like everything too. Harry is here in the kitchen, making a frame for the front of the parlor door. At the time he has fixed the frame so he can work on it tonight putting the paint on it. Looks so naked without it you know. This leaves us all well. Hope this will find you in the best of health. Don't get the blues. Ask Nettie to cheer you up for I know she is lively enough.

I went to Purcellville today and took Rosa to Uncle Kings. She took your waist to Kate to fix it and I took a waist for Ashby for her to make. I saw Stanley pass by the store and smiled at Rosa very sweet. He has only been up once and that was the night she came up. He got here nearly as soon as we did. Came horseback. I suppose Rosa has told you all about him though. Then he went back that night and wrote to her after he got to the depot. I suppose he sleeps there every night and she said he said he was coming up Sunday if he could get off but he did not come. It has been raining nearly all the week. I hope he won't go see her tonight for there is too much bustle there with the babies. Mother is down to Ed's. Him and Laura was up last Sunday and she went home with them. Grandpa told Rosa he was coming up this week but he has not come yet. I suppose the rain prevented him. I don't know. Rosa got a letter from you this evening and she told me you said I could have your hat. I thank you for it but perhaps you will need it yourself. I don't want to deprive you of your hat although I am very much obliged and will take it to Mrs. Silcott as soon as we can go and have it trimmed up.

Well I have sold 2 of the pigs for $2.00 a piece and reckon I can sell the other. Shall I send you the money or keep it here till you come home? I have concluded to let Harry have one out of the five and do with 4 for my meat. I think them as many as I can feed right. Some are so much smaller than others and every body wants the best but won't pay any more for them than they will for the small ones so I just told them they shan't have all the big ones. They have not come for the pigs yet. If he don't come tomorrow I think I will make him pay more. I told Harry you said tend to the sow. He said all right but I would have to send him word when to come. I am giving her Pratt's food and she is heartier than she was.

Well did Rosa tell you C. J. was gone to the city? He has left his mother alone. Claude works up at Enoch, by the month. Says he can't come home every night so we all have to stay by ourselves now. Perry is gone back to Ed, he came home and plowed the lot then went back and told Harry he had to come up and harrow it so he came up night before last and harrowed some yesterday and today a while. It rained so he can't get done. He said Mr. Bean has not planted much corn yet and so he will have to go back down there again before he can finish mine.

Well Lee this is Sunday night and I will try to finish this letter. It has been raining so all the time since Thursday that no one can get about at all it seems. And it has rained more today all day but has ceased a little now. Susie came up yesterday evening with Rosa. Harry took the wagon out there. Rosa and Susie came back in it. She stayed, don't know how long she will stay.

Well I have sold the 3 pigs at $2.00 each comes to $6.00 but, Lee, I owed Mr. Leigh 64c and so I just taken the privilege to take one of your dollars. I will get it for you again as soon as I possibly can. Shall I send you the $6.00 by Rosa? I gave it to her to put in your trunk for fear I might spend it. Said she was not going to put it in there, she was going to spend it but she did not mean it of course. Perry was here this evening. Went back to Ed, said he was going to Wash tomorrow on noon train to Buffalo Bills show. Him and Ed wanted Rosa to give him your address. I suppose he will call on you by the time you get this letter.

Don't you know Dr. Iddings house got burned week before last. I think they saved nearly all the furniture. I never heard of as much burning in my life but his house caught from the kitchen flue. I can't think of any more just now. Hope you are getting along nicely. Write soon with love to you and Nettie I remain your affectionate

Mother

A C sends late kiss

TO: *Miss Ella L. Goode, 11 School St., Mt. Pleasant, Washington, D.C.*

Ellicott City Md.
May 1898

Dear Lee

I will try and write you a short letter tonight. I am sure you have been wondering if I got on that train all right. Well I did. It moved out just as I stepped on. I hope you will pardon me for not thanking you for your kindness. But you may know I appreciated it all very much. I was too excited to do anything right. Just think, if I had been 5 seconds later I would have missed that train. Well I was all right till I reached Relay where I had to change cars. While I was waiting for a connection there it stormed as hard as I ever saw it in my life. There was not much wind but the rain fell in torrents. We could not see fifty yards ahead and when I got to Ellicott City the man had not come to meet me. I was in a fix. I did not know what to do. Finally concluded to hire a carriage and drive over which I did and I suppose I met the man on the way and did not know it. Anyway I got here safe after all and they tried to make me very comfortable. I have everything I could wish except my dear sweet friends to talk with. I spent a very nervous day yesterday. After so much excitement I had one of my crooked days and I have an old waist to work on that is the very mischief and if I work on much longer it will drive me to drink. Well I stop every now and then and pick walnuts which the girls brought up.

I have my dinner served in my room. My breakfast and lunch to take in the dining room. Oh! Lee, I wish you could see this magnificent place. I can not describe it. It will take too much time and space. The grounds are perfectly lovely, something you have read about. I have a bunch of flowers in my room. They have seven peacocks (just so gay), nice milk and butter and the sunshine today was perfect.

After another pick at walnuts I will say, I finished my outing gown and am using it for a wrapper in my room. I have a nice little room all by myself and I am never disturbed after my dinner is served so I washed my corsets this evening after I finished my gown. Well it was rather a hard job. I did not have any ammonia or anything but sweet soap. So considering that I think they look well.

I did nothing like work for myself. I did not feel like it last evening. So I did some writing and went to bed. I wrote to Mama. Hope you have done so too. Did you get work with Mrs. D's friend? I hope so. Do not fail to go to see Mrs. Worch. There will be two or three white dresses. You had better go to see Mrs. Nobles too I think. I have no idea how long I will be out here. I hear them talking about work which sounds like I might sew for a month but I am sure I will not be here that long.

Did you see Cousin Georgianna again? Oh by the way, my trunk did not go out with me after all. I did not get it till yesterday evening.

Thank Mrs. Dellinger for me and tell her I will write to her first opportunity. I have so much writing to do. Tell her to write to me and tell me how she managed the goat this evening. I am sure she found everything all right and no goats to butt her. I know she will like it. Remember to Mr. Dellinger too. I hope the hail did not destroy his garden and flowers after he has toiled so much over them. The hail here broke 890 panes of glass in Mr. McGuire's green house. So you can imagine what it was. It fell at Relay as large as walnuts.

Well I must stop now. I said a short letter but I am sure you will tire of this. Write to me soon and often for I am lonely and tell me have you heard from Maurice. I was dreaming of war last night. How is Mr. G. D.? Give him my love and tell him I say hello. Write something to make me laugh. I don't see any other chance of laughing while I am here. Now goodnight. I am going to bed.

Lovingly

Nettie

Address Ellicott City, Md., c/o Mrs. J. D. McGuire

We have a postman to deliver mail every morning. 3½ miles away from office, isn't that nice.

On back of letter: Mr. S. M. Tramell, Hospital Key West, Florida

TO: *Miss Ella L. Goode, 11 School St., Mt. Pleasant, D.C.*

Postmarked May 7, 1898

MARSHALL COMPANY
506 Fulton Street,
Brooklyn N. Y.

Dear Madam,-

Your reply to our Advertisement is at hand, we want ladies to do work for us at their homes, making our "Perfect Bandage", an article for which there is a large and increasing demand. The work is simple and easy and can be done by any person who can sew a plain seam on a sewing machine—it can be done by girls as well as adults. We pay 25cts. a dozen for making the "Perfect Bandage", and from $2.00 to $3.00 daily can be made after a little practice. Any lady should make at least $2.00 daily by few hours work, even if she cannot devote her whole time to it.

We want lady workers at home to supply our large demands from our many Agents, some of whom are selling 30 to 40 dozen of the Bandages every week and are making large salaries. If you wish to become one of our home workers and give the work a trial, we will send you a complete trial outfit by return mail on receipt of 50 cts. This outfit includes everything necessary to begin work immediately with complete printed instructions. By having our goods manufactured in this way we are enabled to pay much larger wages and our goods cost us less to manufacture because we save the expense of maintaining large and expensive Factories with their never ending expenses for Machinery, Buildings, high rents and other charges which eat up all profits.

After you have filled first trial order and you wish to continue the work, we will refund your deposit of 50 cents for trial outfit, SO IT REALLY COSTS YOU NOTHING TO START. We can supply you with all the work you want to do at home and we pay for each delivery of your work, furnishing all necessary materials for making.

Kindly write us as soon as possible and we trust we can send you a trial outfit. Orders are almost invariably filled same day they are received,—never later than second day. Our correspondence is very large and we aim to be prompt in serving our patrons. If you do not care to give the work a trial please hand this circular to any lady friend who is seeking employment at home.

You can remit money by Post Office Money Order or Express Money Order or if these are not convenient you can send stamps, (in sheets 1c and 2c only.) WRITE YOUR FULL NAME AND ADDRESS PLAINLY and, on receipt of 50 cents, trial outfit and full printed instructions will be sent you at once. We refer you to any Commercial Agency as to our reliability and standing.

Respectfully yours,

The Marshall Company,

506 Fulton St., Brooklyn, N. Y.

TO: *Miss Ella Goode, 11 School St., Mount Pleasant*

FR: The McCall Co., 142-44-46W. 14th St., New York
Postmarked May 14 1898

McCall's Magazine,
GEO. W. YATES, Jr.,
Manager Subscription Dept.
142-146 West 14th Street,
NEW YORK.

New York, May 14th, 1898.

Dear Madam:

Two years ago we had only about two hundred club-raisers. To-day we have nearly three thousand. In order to cover the country, we need at least 8,000 or 10,000, and then each will have plenty of territory, as there were in the United States, 71,022 post-offices, June 30, 1897. We want only one club-raiser in each locality.

Now, if you will send us a list of possible club-raisers in localities other than your own, we will appoint them to represent us, unless the territory is already occupied. In payment for your trouble, you may order one pattern which we will send to you free of charge. Don't send a promiscuous list. Send correct addresses. Return list within ten days after you receive this letter.

If you do as we ask, you will help us circulate the magazine, and that means a better magazine and more profit for you.

Make your list on the back of this sheet.

Yours respectfully,

Geo. W. Yates Jr.

Manager Subscription Department,
"McCall's Magazine."

THE McCALL COMPANY,
142-146 West 14th St., New York.

DEAR SIRS:

Below you will find a list of names of ladies who (I think) might raise clubs for you if you were to send them sample copy and terms to club-raisers.

Name.	Street and Number.	Town.	State.
1			
2			
3			
4			
5			
6			
7			
8			
9			
10			

In payment for my trouble, please send me at once McCALL BAZAR PATTERN No. _____ Size (or Age) _____

Yours truly,

Mrs. or Miss _____

Street and No. _____

Town _____

State _____

SUBSCRIPTION BLANK.

McCall's Magazine.

50 Cents A Year.

Subscriptions to " McCall's "

THE McCALL COMPANY, Publishers,
142-144-146 West 14th Street, New York City, N. Y.

Gentlemen:—Enclosed find $

for ____ Subscriptions to " McCall's "

Magazine " for the Year, at 50 cents each.

_____ 186.

For this Club of ____ Subscribers, please send
me Premium No. ____

Yours respectfully,

____ Solicitor.

Post-Office, ____

County, ____

State, ____

Made, ____

SUBSCRIBERS' NAMES.	STREET OR BOX NO. IF ANY.	POST OFFICE.	COUNTY.	STATE.	Commence Subscription Show with this.

HOW TO REMIT.—Remittances should be made in a Post-Office Money-Order, New York Draft, or an Express Money-Order payable to THE McCALL COMPANY. Where none or these can be procured, send the money in a Registered Letter. Post-Office Money Order Fees——Under $2.50, 3 cents ; $2.50 and less than $5, 5 cents ; $5 and less than $10, 8 cents.

Address all Communications to

THE McCALL COMPANY, 142-146 West 14th St., New York.

33

Postmarked May 14, 1898

> 506 Fulton St., Brooklyn N. Y. May 3/98
> On account of being overcrowded with work your order will be delayed a few days more and we beg your indulgence and patience. We are hurrying orders as rapidly as possible and in a few days expect to catch up and attend to yours
>
> Yours Truly
> Marshall Co

TO: Miss Ella Goode, 11 School St., Mt. Pleasant, Washington, D.C.

Ellicott City, Md
May 26, 1898

Dear Lee,

Your last letter was received. I was glad to hear from you and to hear that you had work. I hope it may continue for you. I did think a few days ago that I could soon be home but things look different now. Miss Mary Merrick sent word that when Mrs. McG. had finished with me she would find something for me to do till the other girls came. Isn't she good to me. But I would like to be in Washington just the same. Well, I have made my black skirt (and don't think very much of it) in my lonely hours. I cut it Sat. night. Basted it Monday. Sewed it Tuesday, put on braid Wednesday and Thursday. I gave it finishing touch, put in a pocket too. Aren't I smart. I have been pidling about. Thought I would cut my red shirtwaist but didn't feel like it. So in a short time I am going to read the Wash. Star to see if I can find any thing about Maurice. Bless his heart.

Did Bertie and the girls come up Sunday? Oh but Sunday was a long old day to me. Just think, I have another to spend here. Oh well, all goes in lifetime. The more lonely I am now, the more company I will have hereafter. Guess I'll have a plenty down there punching fire.

Hope you have heard from home and cousin J is all right. I wonder if I will get up there this summer. Not if I have to pay so much for my room I can't afford to buy a ticket after that. Do you know when I got to Ellicott City I had $1.55 in my purse and it cost $1.25 for a carriage. I had 30 cents left and I have spent the last cent on postage. So this will be the last letter I can write to you until I am paid. Of course if I should stay here three or four weeks it would be just the same. Nobody can rob me now. Oh, by the way that fellow who robbed Dellingers Mansion must have had experience. I never heard of one opening letters before. Tell Mrs. D I can't write to her now till pay day. Well she hears from me through you. I hope she is better now. You must tell me all the news because that is all I know. I have not had my hat on since Friday I came. So you see I'm saving my clothes. We have all had colds. I have been right sick but I am better now. It is very cool and at this moment it is raining and the wind is whistling like winter. Be sure and write so I can get it Monday. I don't know if I will leave here Tuesday or not but don't think I can get through by that time. If you have nothing to do, go down home to see mama. Lee, you don't need any clothes much down there so you can go and wait till I come. Lovingly

Nettie

TO: *Miss Ella Goode, #11 School Street, Mt. Pleasant, Wash, D.C.*

Purcellville, Va.
May 29, 1898

Dear Lee,

I will try and write a very few lines this morning as I am going to Purcellville so of course I can't have time to write much this time but will write more next time. This leaves us all well except granma. She is complaining a great deal with her side. When she was thrown out of Ed's buggy about 2 weeks ago as she was coming home she fell on the wheel and she must have broken a rib, but I don't know. She goes about all the time but not able to do much but never is you know.

Hope this will find you quite well and in better spirits, as I hear you have heard from the absent one that went to Cuba so I guess you are lively now as he is on the mend from his sickness. It is very bad for him but I guess he is safer there than on a boat on the water.

Well Lee, I must thank you kindly for my dress as I appreciate it very much indeed. I am going up to get Lula to cut it for me this evening and I may get Kate to help me to make it. You better come up to church Sunday and show yourself as you know it is show day. I expect Miss Fletcher and Bert that day, also Kate. Cinda says they are coming Saturday of course. Kings too and Rosa said Arthur, you know he will eat up all if he comes. Well, Lee, your old Isaiah has not been here but once for 3 months, I think that was the night before Rosa went down, has forsaken us.

Harry took the sow down and kept her 3 or 4 days. Now she is back. She is beginning to look better. I tell you I was uneasy about her sometime ago. She did not eat enough to keep her alive but she is all right now.

Give my love to Blanche when you see her as I have not time to write to her this morning and tell her I thank her for my birthday present. I had forgotten I had a Birthday until I got my present. I hope she is satisfied and will do all right. Well Lee, I have to stop for the horse is waiting and I must get ready. Rosa has written to you also. Guess she has told you all. Will say goodbye with all of our love to you and I do send love and kiss, Lee.

You must write to me whenever you can. Your loving,

Mama

Purcellville, Va.
May 31st 1898

Dear Lee,

I will seat myself with pleasure this morning to write you a few lines which I hope you will accept. I arrived safe Sunday on the noon train. I found after I got to Falls Church that there was no trains running up here in the afternoon on Sundays so I had 10 minutes to wait so I did not get to see any one in Falls Church. The electric cars were jammed and steam train also. I thought I would be mashed up when I got out. As I was crossing from the electric car station to the steam cars I met a soldier. He was about as tall as Maurice. He had black hair and mustache, said "Hello sister." I smiled in return to his remark. After a spell he came over to the station again and as I started to get on the train he asked me if I was going to leave then. I said yes, he asked how far. I told him away up in Loudoun. He said Is that all.

Ma is very much pleased with her dress. Thinks it lovely. Walter said he thanked you very much for his studs. Mr. Cooksey came to the car with me. Said he was going to Georgetown anyway.

I left Blanche so mad that I don't know whether a letter would be acceptable from me or not. She made me so infernal mad (pardon expression) I could have beat her. She hasn't as much sense as a fool.

She set there and bellowed like some little baby and it was all because I would not go with her up to see old Clarence Seaton. She saw him Thursday and she heard he had mashed his foot very bad and she was crazy to see him. She said she asked me to go Saturday evening and I would not do it. Said I was expecting company. Said any time she said she was going to have company I always said didn't make any difference. Well I did expect company and I was not going away when I knew they were coming and after I had started down the street she called me back upstairs. I went up and she wanted me to wait until eve and take her up to see him and because I would not do it she struck up another howl. If he isn't here every day she wants to go see him, she must have it bad.

Clara is pleased to death over her ring. I sent Nora hers by Perry Sunday night. Lee there is to be flag raising tonight. You ought to be here. All are well and send love. Write soon,

Rosa

I saw Stanley as I got off the train. He tipped his hat and asked how long I was going to stay up. I told him I didn't know and I didn't guess he cared, so he walked on.

TO: *Miss Ella L. Goode, No. 11 School Street, Mt. Pleasant, Washington, D.C*

Dynard P.O.
June 23, 1898

Dear Friend,

Your letter received and read with much pleasure, was glad to hear from you. Also glad to hear you are coming down soon. I would have written before but I am always sick. Sorry to say I am never well. I wrote to you last week but was taken sick and never sent it. I am little better now. I surely have had a hard time of it. Since Christmas I have been in bed three times. Since then my doctor bill was 19 dollars and half.

I hope this letter will find you well. Now Lee, do come down. I think it would do me lots of good for I do stay home so much I get downhearted. If I had someone to go about with I think it would do me good. You said something about not coming. Why not come? I am sure everyone would be glad to see you. I am very sure I would. You said everyone got disgusted with Rosa. I did not for I did not see her long enough to get acquainted with her. I never saw any harm in Rosa. Now Lee, don't let that stop you from coming down for who would blame you for what Rosa did if she had done anything. I never heard anyone say much about her.

Cora's baby has been sick. Had the doctor to it but it is getting all right now. Sissie has another daughter, soon be two weeks old. Little Ella has two teeth. She was four months old day before yesterday. Little Elmer has been wearing pants but he has a dress on today. He looks funny in pants. Rose came to see me when I was sick. Georgy came up two or three times, came in the house to see how I was. I see Cora every day. She is well. Lee, write me soon and tell me when you are coming down. If you want to come to my house first write me word and Webster will meet you at the wharf. Well, as I have no more to say at present I will bring my short letter to a close with much love to you I remain a true friend,

Emma Good

TO: Miss Ella Goode, #11 School Street, Mount Pleasant, D.C.

Postmarked Falls Church
June 24, 1898

Dear Ella

Did you know that Mr. Appich was married? And gone to the war. And his father drives the candy wagon for him. Walter has written to us from Florida and I must close now being as I have something else on my mind that I mustn't lose time in doing it.

Ethel R. Gordon

Maddox P.O., St. Mary's Co., Md.
July 5, 1897 (Postmarked 1898)

My dear Niece,

Your kind and ever welcome letter came duly at hand yesterday (Monday) and was very glad to hear from you. I had not forgotten you but had commenced to think you had forgotten me. I would love to see you, trust you will come down instead of going home. You have been home so often since you were down here. Everybody seems anxious to see you. I was greatly disappointed when the boys came home Christmas when I found that you did not come.

Well so far as you thinking anything about Gus not coming to see you it is useless for Gus cares for no one but herself and she does not seem to care much about herself. It is not only hot down here for tis terrible dry. There has been one or two slight showers today but not enough to do much good. We have a very poor crop this year, the worst crop we have made since we have been living at Notly Hall. You need not be afraid to come down on account of war for there is no danger traveling on boat now. It is perfectly safe. Julia and her husband cannot stay in this house another year. They will have to go to themselves. Lee, I can tell you that you were not the only one that was surprised for there were a great many that were not only surprised but were angry with Julia for marrying him.

Well Uncle Jim sends his love to you. Jimmie was here Sunday. He was looking very badly. He has been in bad health for 2 wk. He is sailing with Captain Framton, has been on board the vessel ever since April.

Well, I must close. Hoping you will come down soon. I will close with love to you from all the family. I remain

Your devoted aunt

J. Goode

P.S. Please excuse bad writing and mistakes. I am in a large hurry. Come down soon. Write soon.

E. B. GOODE,

Blacksmith, Wagons Made to Order,

<small>Dealer in</small>

Hardware * and * Farm * Implements.

BATTLE FOR LIFE
THE RETAIL
MERCHANTS'

Aldie, Va.,

Aldie, Va.
July 17th, 1898

Dear Friend,

Your most welcome letter was recd in due time. I was more than glad to hear from you. I hope you are well as it leaves us all better Mary was quite sick last week but is getting better now. The baby is growing some but he is still small. Well what have you been doing with yourself? This warm weather it surely has been terrible. We are having a lovely rain tonight which will be such a great help to the gardens as they are all drying up so. Well Lee, do you hear from home often? None of them has been down but I guess they are always busy like we are. Are you coming home before Bush meeting? Let me know. If so we will come up to Bush meeting and bring you back with us and go from here to camp meeting. Is George coming up this Summer? Look here, what is the matter with you and George? I surely am wanting to see you. I miss you so much, wish you were here tonight. Wouldn't we talk. I guess I will be an old maid but I don't want you to be one too. Well how is Rosa and where is she now? Mary is always writing to cousin Lee but never gets it finished. Well isn't the Summer flying but there is the old saying time waits for no man. How is Nettie? Give my love to her and say I hope she is well. Tell her to come up to see us.

Well all have gone to bed and by the looks of this writing I ought to be there too. I went to hear Mr. Camel preach this morning. I got so hot and sleepy. I had to turn and twist much to keep from going to sleep. Love from your true friend

Maude

Wash, D.C.
July 24, 98

Dear Miss Goode,

I will now try to answer your very welcome letter and which was very gladly received. I certainly was glad to hear that you had such a pleasant time. I am so tired today. I don't know what to do. Nellie, Mama, Mr. Brinkman and myself all went down the river to River View last night and we didn't get home until half past twelve. Frank couldn't go for Saturday is such a busy day and he couldn't have gotten home in time. When we got home (Frank came to meet us) we found Nev and Miss Simpson almost asleep. She came on the 9 o'clock train and so he didn't like to leave her alone so he waited until we came and he was so tired and sleepy he had to stay all night.

Miss Nettie says she expects to go to Purcellville next Monday, and I have made up my mind to go up home with Nellie next Sunday and stay two weeks. Cal is up there now and he will buy my ticket when I come and so it won't cost me but half fare. Well what do you think. I will tell you something you must keep mum about it. Nev is going home in two weeks and we are afraid to be married. He has looked at a house over on 15th street that he always said he would like to have so much, for it has an acre of ground around it and so it is for rent and he is trying his best to get it. But another party has spoken for it so maybe he won't be fortunate enough to get it. But he says if he can get it he will and sew turnips, and of course he will get married then sooner than he expected. But don't say anything to anybody for he may not want everybody to know it.

I am so glad Maurice is getting better. He may get to hear out of both ears—who knows.

Well I will soon have to commence dinner. I wish you was here to help eat it. Oh yes, Miss Nichols was up last Sunday and wanted to know when you was coming back. She said she would like to have you sew for her for two days. Well I made my other dress and a white skirt last week. I got a cheap wrapper the other day and I am going to get Miss Nettie to help me make it for I have only got this week and so much to do. I would be glad to see you before I go away if you could come out. If you can't come out write and let me know how you are. Well goodbye. With love, I remain your Friend,

Mrs. D.

Washington, D.C.
July 24th 98

Dear Lee,

Your letter received in Ellicott City. I arrived home last night about 9 o'clock. Mrs. D. and Nellie had gone down the river and Mr. D. had gone to meet them. Mr. N.M.D. was at the house waiting for me. He stayed with me until they came. Isn't he good to me? I act mean with him sometimes though. I will have work here a few days, then I will get myself ready for Purcellville. I am going up Monday eve Aug 1st. Will be there for Bush meeting. I am sorry you will not be there. As you are not there I will go to cousin Kingsley. I wish I did not have to take my trunk. But I would not have anything fit to wear if I pack things closely. I wish you would come in before I go. I want to talk with you so much. You and Carl come in some evening or next Sunday. Or Maurice if he is there. Remember me to him.

Do you know I went to church this morning and I am going again this evening. It is very pleasant today and nothing like being at home again. I have had a lonely time of it this summer and this summer is almost over too.

I have nothing to write of any importance so I will close now. Hoping you are having a nice time and remain with love,

Your fond cousin

Nettie

Purcellville, Virginia
July 26th 98

Dear Lee,

Your letter rec'd some days past and I have not had a chance to answer. I have been to Uncle Kingsley's a few days, was on my way there when I got your letter. Stayed there until Monday eve. Tuesday morning I went to Mollie's to help her thresh wheat and just came home today (Thursday) and am now head over heels in work. But had a fine time today. Best time I have had for a spell. Had a house full of company all day and most of them were your old chums (you know the word chum means much). We had a fine time, about raised Cain about here. One of the guests was Mr. Beans. Every time we mentioned your name they made strange of it. Said they had forgotten there ever was a girl named Lee. As I began naming the guests I continue doing so although I do not intend to ever try to name them all for it would take all the paper in Loudoun County. Clarence Davis, Rozzel D., Dickson Hospital and Wade Palmer from Unison and others too numerous to mention.

I had a letter from Joe on my return home. I found it awaiting my return. Bush meeting will soon be here. I suppose you are coming up. I heard Mama say you were coming Saturday or Monday if it is convenient. I would like you to let me know for sure which day you are coming and on what train. You ought to come Saturday for the meeting over here is Sunday. Is anyone coming with you? I mean (M). Elton Seaton is over to Mrs. Seaton's now. Expects to go back Saturday or Monday, wants to try and stay up until Monday if possible. But is compelled to come home.

Well I must close as I am in a hurry to post it. So will say "Au, Revoir"

Your Little Sister

HaHaHa Rosa

Let me know when to meet you if possible for when I meet the train so many times people say I just come there to see Stanley Smith and he will think the same. I must avoid going there any more than possible. Bye. Don't laugh too much. "yes, that's so?" What's so sa sartan, Laugh no, Don't laugh.

E. B. GOODE,
Blacksmith, Wagons Made to Order,
Dealer in
Hardware * and * Farm * Implements.

BATTLE FOR LIFE
THE RETAIL
MERCHANTS'

Aldie, Va.,
FARM MACHINERY PRINT, FOR SUBSCRIBER

Aldie, Va.
Aug 1st, 1898

My dear Old Friend,

Your most welcome missive recd in due time. I was more than glad to rec it, if it was short and sweet. Now I do hope you will have a gay time at Bush meeting.

Mr. Goode is not at all well. Was quite sick yesterday in bed but is up today. So, Lee, I guess it will be doubtful about us getting up to Bush meeting. But will come up the end of the week if all's better and you see the meeting will be over then and we will come in the carriage so you can come back with us. As you see you must come before you go to see Cousin George for when you go I'm afraid you won't come back.

Little Nellie often dresses up and starts to Aunt Mag's but you see she don't get all the way. Lee, Sister Lizzie is now at Forest Hotel Franconia, New Hampshire, and is having quite a gay time. Says it is lovely there. It is a great summer place to go. She thinks she will be benefited quite much by it. Well, Lee, I am like you were when you wrote, so sleepy. All join in best love to one and all. Goodbye.

Your True Friend,

Maude Ellison

45

Hillsboro, Va.
Aug 9, 1898

Miss Good

Doubtless you will be somewhat surprised in receiving this letter, probably you may ridicule it. However I am going to send it and trust you will receive it in the same kindly manner in which it is written.

No excuse no apology can I offer for my boldness, other than the friendship which has existed since the short interview the last time I saw you.

Hope you had a pleasant stay in the country. Your mother told me you expected to return to the city the 8th and I do not know your address. However I will just send it to Purcellville and let it find you.

I was anxious to see you at the Bush Meeting but was deprived of the opportunity. But when I am disappointed I find consolation in the poet's words "there'll come a time some day." Hoping you will not render my letter audacious, but deem it worthy of a reply. I remain Respt.

Robt. G. Jenkins

Friday Morning, Aug 19 1898

Dear Ella Lee,

In compliance with your request, I will write you a few lines although I hardly have time now as I have been going to Camp most every day and am tired entirely out and am going again Sunday if nothing prevents. Mr. Jay, Harry, Kate and myself went up Saturday. Spent the night with Jim, came back Sunday. Tuesday Groom took me up again and then who do you think took me up Thursday? Was quite a surprise to me, Wednesday night a "sporty" fellow came up here and asked me to go up with him Thursday. I jumped at the idea. He is to take me Sunday too. It is Stanley. He just got a new buggy and a horse. I teased him about Lillie Burke. He said he found those girls too fast for him. Walter Benedum wanted me to go up Wednesday with him but I would not go. Clarence is going to take Nettie and myself both up tomorrow (Saturday). Nettie has been to Ed's since Tuesday and is coming up here today again. We came very near getting our necks broke that day Monday. We went to Ed's and no one was home but Perry so we stayed all the evening and got our suppers. Had a picnic.

I had a lovely time with Wade Palmer and Dickson H at Camp last Sunday. I tell you he is a warm number in fact, is the warmest thing that ever happened. ("Now will you be good.")

What kind of a time are you having? A Billy goat time or a Poll Parrot time? I guess a Billy goat time. Mrs. Rea and Lula started home Thursday. Mr. Strait is at Atlantic City and did not expect her home until Saturday. She gave me the quarter she owed you. Said she had forgotten it entirely but I have it all right. Now it is in good hands when it gets in mine. By the way have you seen Joe yet? He is in Charles Co. I hope he is/will keep away from St. Mary's.

Saw John Bodmer Thursday at Camp, asked if you had gone to Washington. Said Maude Ellison had been up the country and fell off the fence and broke her arm.

Ma says she will write as soon as she can. I say not to stay in the room so much and get the fever. Ha.

I had another letter from Groome the other day. He is clear dead gone. But he can't help it and I don't care too. Susie and Blanche went home with Ruth and are now homesick crazy to come home. I wrote we were coming after them Wednesday. After Wednesday I am going to say we had other business and would come next week, just to keep them over there long as can. Bye Bye, write soon,

Hastily
All join in love,

Rosa

Wash. D.C.
Aug 30, 98

Miss Goode,

Dear Friend, I recd your letter and was very glad indeed to hear you are having such a delightful time. But I am afraid if you stay much longer poor Maurice won't be any where.

Well I must tell you the news. Harry and Lizzie Spiker was married last Monday a week ago and Frank has rented the rooms and comes here the 15th and starts for house keeping. Little did I think of such a thing when I last wrote you. I certainly was surprised. You said you did not know when you was coming back. Well I bet you will be the next one to step off for I know that heavy baud ring don't mean nothing. Well I am sorry you can't be with me this winter, but maybe Mrs. Lanham can give you and Miss Simpson a nice room.

Well when you come don't fail to come and see me and in the meantime if I hear of any body wanting sewing done I will let you know. Well I haven't time to write you much for I ought to be getting supper now. Excuse poor writing as in haste. Mr. D. sends his best regards, hoping to hear from you real soon. I remain your Friend

Mrs. Dellinger

Purcellville Virginia
Sept 1st, 1898

Dear Ella,

It is with pleasure that I seat myself this evening to write you a few lines to let you know I am still on the land among the living and am not stopped going yet as Arnold Grove has a picnic tomorrow Thursday and the Chapel Saturday. We are going on straw ride down there at night. Sam is going to get Enich's wagon.

Frank is up, came up Saturday on noon train. Nettie has been to Purcellville for a week, came back Tuesday eve and we have just been having a sporty time. You missed lots by not going to Camp.

Mr. Beans was up Sunday but I did not see him very long as I went to bed and slept until supper then dressed and went to Purcellville meeting. The meeting begins here Sunday the first. I guess you will be here by that time, will you not? I mean before it closes. Look here Lady, you had just better stop going with Sol so much. It might accidentally on purpose lead to matrimony and Sol is my little "mash." He is the warmest thing that ever happened. I lost my heart when I first saw him. I know I haven't seen him for nearly a year, but you shan't have him, no you shall not. I will fight first. Now you got it?

Well, well don't you think Stanley and I have had another quarrel and all is ended now so Janney and I are good friends once more. He isn't afraid of his father for he is the one taken me to church Sunday night. Perry taken Nettie in a livery buggy, brought her up here Sunday eve and then went to church and left her at Uncle Kingsley's that night until Tuesday.

There is no need for you to send your love to Mr. Beans for he is through with your foolishness and believe it or not he has found a wife at last from Farmwell. I have never seen her and people say she is only a little over seventeen years old. He is to be married, I think some time this month. So Burr is moving out. Mollie was about to fight him. He and Harry were up last night. Nettie and I went for a drive, did not get back until nine.

I am going to send this letter to Maddox as you said you were going to Uncle Jim's. Tell Uncle Jim his boy is all right and longs to see his Daddie once again.

Tell Jennie I certainly could not answer her letters, she wrote so many it frightened me too bad.

Old Bert Grubb died last Saturday and had to sit up with her Orra, Mary, Sam and Claude. There was not anyone to do a thing so we sat up Saturday night, was buried Sunday morning. They were but few at the funeral here, they buried her in Lovettsville. They asked me to sing a piece at the house so I sang Nearer My God To Thee at their request. I was glad enough to sing for she isn't only better off but other people too.

I must close my scribbling this time, awaiting a quick reply. Give my love to all at Uncle Jim's, also Dixi's. So bye bye. Love,

I remain your Darling

Rosa

September 20th 1898
Maddox P.O.

My Dearest

Friend, I will take this pleasure in writing you a few lines to let you hear from me but I don't guess that you care to hear from me, but I want to hear from you and would have written to you before this if I had known where to write. But I never knew until last night. They got a letter from you and they told me where to write and I thought that it would not cost me much to write to you even if you did not answer it.

Well now my old sweetheart you said that Wilson got to the wharf but I did not get there and you said that I did not want to come, if I had I would have gotten there. But I hope that you just said that just fore to vex me because you would not believe that I loved you, but you don't know how bad it was to me to see you going so far away from me. I could not do anything but wave to you. Could not even speak a word to you but I guess that there will come a time some day when we are together again.

Well Jennie told me that you were very mad with me that Friday night because I would not come in the house and you know that it was nothing to get mad about. I told her that I did not think that you were mad with me about that because if you had been mad with me you would not have let me kiss you good night. And if I had known that I would not see you any more Dicksie would not have gotten me away from you as soon as he did. Well now I guess that it is all right now because it made me feel so sorry to get so close and get disappointed. But I love you the best of all the girls that I know. I would like to be with you today.

It is blowing very hard and I can't write. Well I will have to stop writing fore this time. I am so nervous that I can't write and I guess that you will get tired of reading this. I remain as ever your loving friend

J R C

Remember me when this you see
Sealed with a kiss but I have had none

E. B. GOODE,
Blacksmith, Wagons Made to Order,
<small>Dealer in</small>

Hardware * and * Farm * Implements.

B<small>ATTLE FOR LIFE
THE RETAIL
MERCHANTS'</small>E

Aldie, Va.,.
<small>FARM MACHINERY PRINT. FOR BUSINESS</small>

Aldie, Va.
Sept 23, 1898

My dear Lee,

Yours to hand tonight. Glad you are home again and I hope you will be able to come down before you leave. I am in a big hurry tonight as Ed and I are going to Washington and will be back on Monday eve. We will come up on the train that gets to Purcellville at 7 o'clock so if you will come down to Leesburg we can bring you out Monday night. Come if you can. I want you to help me do some sewing if you can. I have had quite a time of it this summer. Have had so much to do. I want to go to Purcellville some time this fall and stay a while with your mother and Mrs. Davis. I have not been anywhere since last summer. Only to see Brother once when he was so sick but glad to say he is better now. Tell Mag we looked for her until our eyes are sore but I hope she will come yet this fall. I know she has a poor chance to leave. Mother came down to stay and take care of the baby while I took a little trip.

Love to all, now be sure to come if you can and if you don't get this in time to come on Monday come some other day and come out on the stage and I will pay the staging. Now be sure and do it. Maude's arm is better but has not got the board off yet. I must say good night. With love to all

Yours devotedly

Eliza Goode

Merrifield
Sept 30, 98

My Dear Friend,

I will hasten to answer your welcome letter I received yesterday. I was glad to hear from you and we were also glad to hear Miss Sallie was coming to see us and you must be sure and stop too for a while. You said you were coming to see us again last winter but you did not come. I would love dearly to come to visit you but it is of no use to talk of going anywhere this year, for as you know the soldiers have been camping all around us all this summer so that we could not get away from home. And now that they are all gone we are going to have another little kick up. "Eddie" (my brother who is in Baltimore) is to be married the 2nd of November and will be here with his bride about the middle I guess. And we are also building an addition on to our house, so you see we have been a little upset all the time.

Tell Miss Sallie she must be sure and come prepared to stay until after the bride and groom get here. Tell her to get off the train at Dunn Loring and we will meet her there and you too. It is only about a mile and a half to the station.

You ask where was Aunt Jennie. She is now nursing Harvey Kirby with the typhoid fever. He is very low. There is a great deal of sickness around here this fall especially of fever. Caused I suppose by the camp.

Mamma says she would love to come to see you all, and will before long. Tell your ma to come to see us. We do not live so very far away.

Well I will bring this uninteresting letter to a close. All send love to you all. Write soon and be sure to come. I remain your friend.

May H. Richards

P.S. Mamma sends her love to your grandmother and says for her to come down with you, she would love to see her. Be sure to send us word before you come.

Hillsboro Va.
Oct 2, 1898

Miss Goode,

Esteemed friend, I received your long looked for letter at last and with it came much pleasure for I had come to the conclusion that you had blotted me out of your memory forever. But according to the old adage "the darkest hour is just before the dawning."

I hoped to have an opportunity to see you before you went back to the city but it seems as if Providence will not permit.

Will you be at the picnic at Short Hill? I expect to be there and would be delighted to see you if you have no other engagement. I had the pleasure of seeing your mother at the picnic at James Chapel but was sorry it was not you.

I will bring my short letter to a close with the request that you excuse my fancy paper. I am

Yours Very Respt.

Robt. G. Jenkins

Maddox P.O.
Oct 5, 1898

Dear Lee,

Your letter rec'd and very glad to hear from you. This leaves me in very bad health and do not get any better. I hope this scribbling reaches you. It may find you well and having a gay old time. Lee, George came up here the Sunday after you left and was up again last Sunday again. He is looking fine, just as fat as a jockey and is quite lively. You asked me what time Mr. Goode got home. He went by Sophia's to carry her a piece of beef and got home about 9 o'clock. He had plenty on board when he got here.

Jim said he was just 5 minutes too late. He said he waved at the boat until it was out of sight. Said he would like to have been there 5 min. sooner. Nettie come back here last Sat. and we went to Church and from there we went to Mr. Higgs and spent the day. Sam carried Nettie up to Mechanicsville Wednesday. I sent Nettie down to Sophia's on Monday to carry a piece of lamb. We had a pulling feast and could not leave. She said she was up and she thought she was eating too much. Well Jennie and Nettie went up to Mr. Graves and Nettie made a mash on Mr. Graves. They are rather nice looking boys. Well I have told you all the news only I forgot to say that Fanny and her husband were down and Fanny thought very hard of them for not coming down to see her.

Well must now close with love from all the family and myself in particular. I remain

Your loving aunt

J. Goode

Remember me to Aunt Cinda and Uncle Kings. Tell them I am glad that they are all right. Did you all get frightened before you got to the wharf or did your Uncle Jim slacken his mule's speed? I hope he did. By bye, J. Goode

TO: *Miss Ella L. Goode, 815 22nd St., N.W., Washington, D.C.*

Aldie Va.
Postmarked Nov 8, 1898

Dear Cousin Lee,

How are you? Have you got a place? The meeting broke up Tuesday. Mary says write to her soon. All send love. Mama went to Halfway Friday and papa went after her today. I have been to church. We are going to prayer meeting tonight. The Professor is coming to fix Aunt Maude's organ tomorrow. Write sometime. Miss Blanche Carruters was baptized today. Aunt Maude says write her sometime. I miss you so much.

Annie C. Goode

Well dear Lee,

Annie has told you all the news and left none for me, but will write a little bit. Was glad to see your letter but so sorry you had such a time. Hope you are all right now. I seen John at church Sunday eve and he had his bow on and it looked real cute. I made it last week and Eliza was going down town so she taken it and told him some girl sent it to him. He over taken us Sunday night going to prayer meeting. I told him I had heard from you and he wanted to know how you were. I told him you still had the Head Ache. That you couldn't of stayed longer. He seemed sorry. He told me he had worn his bow Sunday eve. I did not tell him of your accident. Thought maybe I had better not. Have you heard from him yet? Or have you wrote now? Mind what I say you must be good to him.

Well Lee, the meeting soon closed after you left. I surely did enjoy the meeting, Lee. Eliza was so out done when we came home and found Mr. Goode had not given you anything. So she sends you order for $3.00. Hope you will get plenty to do and get along nicely. Eliza says she will make the balance all right when you come up Xmas. I tell you the time will soon pass away and I know John will be glad. Mr. John Bodmer has not rung the doorbell for some time and we miss it. Tom was working here today fixing the porch. Mr. Goode has fixed the front walk and it looks real nice. Nellie says Cousin Lee come back here now. I tell, Mary's birthday was yesterday. Now write real soon and a long letter to your good Friend

Maude Ellison

Miss Kate is improving. I surely hope she will recover.

TO: *Miss E. L. Goode, 815 22nd St. N.W., Washington, D.C.*

Aldie Va.
Nov 16th, 1898

Miss E. L. Goode,

Dear Friend,

I received your very welcome letter Monday evening and will write one day sooner than I did last week. I have just come from Mr.

Wrenn's store and will have some spare time so I will entertain myself writing and as I enjoy writing to nobody else better than I do writing to you. I expect the time will pass very rapidly. It is raining again. It seems like it rains every time I write to you but I don't reckon that is the cause of it because it was raining before I commenced to write. When I read your letter and came to the place where you said you were writing before breakfast I thought you must be an earlier riser than I am or else you must have late breakfast on Sunday for I can't hardly get up in time for breakfast on Sunday and if it wasn't for Sunday School I don't expect I would get any breakfast at all on Sunday.

So you think Miss Maude told me about your fall, but you are mistaken about that for Miss Maude never told me a word about it. But I expect she told the one that told me, my brother Tom. I guess you know he was working up to Mr. Goode's and he heard it up there and told me but he didn't know much about how it happened.

I saw Miss Jordan over to the store this evening. She is very anxious to know if you write to me or not. She asked me if I would answer a question if she asked me. I told her it depended on what the question was. So she asked me when I had heard from you. I didn't know what answer to give so I just laughed and told her I hadn't heard from you at all only what Miss Maude had told me. She said she was going to write to you this week so I suppose you have her letter before this. She came from uptown tonight when I was over to the store and had a package of candy but she said she didn't buy it. She offered us all some for she said she had eaten as much as she wanted.

I had a long talk with my friend Mrs. Moore last Sunday. I had started to church and a gentleman came along and asked me to step in and ask Mrs. Moore to come to the door. So I stayed there and had quite a talk with her. I told her I had heard that I was putting on a lot of style. She said she hadn't heard anything of that. Her memory must be short. I went to Christian Endeavor at night but it was so dark and rainy there wasn't but a few there so didn't have any meeting. I asked you in my last letter if Eddie Watson had been down to the city but you didn't say anything about it when you wrote so I suppose he hasn't been down yet. I guess George will be up to see you before long. Think it real nice of him to send you box of flowers. If he comes to Washington give him my kindest regards.

There have been three weddings near here today. One was in Aldie at Mr. Badger's. They were people from Oatlands. The other

John W. Bodmer

two were up near Mountsville and Philomont. The meeting at Presbyterian Church is to begin next Sunday morning. There will be lots
of preachers here that day. Three sermons, two of them Presbyterian
and one at the Methodist Church. Would like very much for you to
be here to attend the meeting but I know it is impossible for you to
come. I guess I can find some boys to go to church with. I would like
to come down to the city before Christmas but don't expect I will be
able to get off as we are very busy in the shop and Christmas is coming so fast. I am getting sleepy and the clock is just striking ten so I
guess I will have to stop scribbling this nonsense. I suppose you
haven't moved yet. If you have I suppose of course you will let me
know when you write. Think it would be much nicer to be with your
cousin though of course you know best about that. Suppose you went
to Mt. Vernon Church last Sunday. Hope you liked the preacher and
also enjoyed your dinner with your friend.

Trusting to hear from you real soon. I am as ever your sincere
friend,

J. W. B.

Aldie Va.
Nov 23rd 1898

Miss E. L. Goode,

Dearest friend,

I have just come home from church and sit down to write. It is getting late and I will have to write rapidly and so you must excuse bad writing for I know before I commence that I will not do very plain writing when I am in a hurry. I hope you will get this sooner than you got the last one. I thought perhaps you had moved before I wrote to you but I couldn't do anything but send it to your old address.

Well as I said at the beginning I have just come home from church. They have an Evangelist to hold the meeting. He is an old man and doesn't speak very loud so I don't expect Mr. Douglass can hear him. I like him tolerably well but he is not what I expected he would be. I had heard so much about him before he came. I was out to hear him last night. It was raining and there were only about a dozen people there. He preached about prayer last night and tonight again and Sunday evening. Mr. Stanton preached on the same subject. So I have heard a good deal about prayer in the last three or four days. And that reminds me that you asked in your last letter to be remembered in my prayers and I will say that I do pray for you. I was about to say every day but I fear that I forget some days.

There is to be a special Thanksgiving service in Middleburg at the Methodist Church tomorrow night. I have been thinking about going but don't know for sure whether I will go or not. If you were here and would go with me it wouldn't take me long to make up my mind. I have been very fortunate in having some of the boys go to church with me every night so far, but it doesn't seem natural to go with boys since I got used to going with you at our meetings. I suppose you are enjoying yourself in your new home. I hope so at least. I would like very much to come down to the city between this and Christmas but don't know if I can or not. Certainly not under two weeks. If the weather is not too bad in two or three weeks I may be able to come down for a day or two and you may rest assured that if I do come you will see me if I can find you.

I saw Eddie Watson two or three days ago and he told me he hadn't been down to the city yet but he expected to go right soon. I see Miss Jordan once in a while and she most always tells me something that you said in your letter to her but of course I know she is only joking as you said you hadn't heard from her at all. She has been to church every night. John Hensley and Lew keep turns going with her. Her friend Charlie from Upperville was down Sunday and spent the day.

You said something about not being sure of coming up here Christmas but I hope it will be so you can come and I am going to keep on expecting you to come anyhow and as Annie says why don't you come. I reckon I had better close as it is getting late and I am getting sleepy. Expecting to hear from you on Monday for I believe you always write on Sunday. I am as ever your true friend

J. W. B.

TO: *Miss Ella L. Goode, No. 815-22 St., N.W., Washington, D.C.*

Lincoln, Va.
Nov 28th, 1898

My dear Ella,

Your letter which arrived a few weeks ago was much appreciated. I had begun to wonder where you were and whether you ever intended writing to me again. I was very glad to be assured by your nice letter that you occasionally thought of me. Now I know you do not have much time to spend many thoughts on me for your many admirers claim most of your thoughts. I do think you are the most fortunate and the most unfortunate girl I ever saw. Scarcely lose one fellow before you have another. How do you manage it? I declare you are becoming quite a belle. What did you do to Maurice? I am glad to know your last "catch" is so nice. I do wonder if I could think he is as nice as Mr. D-.

Lucie delivered your pears. I can assure you that he did not think you one bit bold, but appreciated your kindness so very much and told us to tell you that he was very much obliged to you for them. Yes I ate a piece of one. I pared it for him and then I claimed a little piece.

Wasn't that right? I don't wonder that Mr. Bobbie "stopped short, never to go again" if he had heard what I did. Not many weeks ago I heard that Miss Ella Goode and Mr. Beans were to be married. You are real mean for not telling me all about it when I was out to see you. I certainly thought you honored me enough to have me for one of your maids. Tell me all about it when you write. Poor Bobbie, was no wonder he don't write. Perhaps he will send some arbutus for the occasion. I expect his heart is almost broken but perhaps he has sympathy from some of his favorite poets.

I am glad to know that you had such a pleasant visit at Aldie and Eddie called to see you. Tripping through the streets of Aldie that night went Eddie and Ella to Church. Poor girl and she sent him word not to come. Ella, I think that is pretty bad. Last Saturday we had the first snow of the season. It snowed in good earnest for some time but soon melted. Sunday was a very cold windy day but I went down to Hughesville and had quite a fine time. Besides the home folks, Alice Watson, Lee Laycock, Mr. Demory and I were there. Don't say we didn't have a jolly good time. Alice and Eddie came up to our house last Saturday week. Alice spent a few days with us. Do you know Claude Saffer? He's to marry the sixth of next month. Miss Ollie Riticor is the young lady he is to marry. I expect that Leslie and William's wedding will be quite a stylish affair. I would like very much to go, but do not think I can. I suppose you have heard all about it as it is to take place so near your home.

Nettie Nichols and John Warner were married last week. I wonder if you will get tired of reading this long letter, but I want to tell you all the news.

You asked me what success they had at Trinity. Five were converted and united with the Church. I was one of the number. Mr. Wolfe is now conducting a meeting at Hamilton. Thirty have been converted.

We expected to have an entertainment at Trinity Xmas, but have for the present given up the idea. It is so hard for Trinity to have anything. One reason that we did not have it was on account of whooping cough being in the neighborhood. There is now talk of having an Epworth League Social. Don't know what kind of an affair that will be. I do hope they will have something for it is going to be so quiet in this neighborhood at that time. I wish I could spend Xmas in Washington again but that will be impossible. Are you looking forward to a pleasant time?

I have had my new dress made for some time. I succeeded in getting the kind of velvet that I wanted through the kindness of Miss Sallie Downs who was at that time in Baltimore. The narrow green velvet I thought was very cheap; 26 cents for ten yards. I put nearly ten yards on the skirt and two on the waist. Had a green velvet front and yoke of the velvet in the back. So you can imagine I am quite green.

We killed hogs today. So we are living in Greece for a while. Not a very desirable place. Is Rosa in Washington yet? How is Nettie? Give her my best love.

Do you ever see Alma and Alice Boucher? I have not had a letter from them for some time. Someone told me that the Kirby boys (all except Ray) had had the typhoid fever this Fall and one of them had died. It wasn't the one that they called Ward was it? I met him whilest at Langley and thought him quite pleasant.

You ought to go out to Langley some time. I am quite sure you would enjoy it. I so often think of the pleasant time I had there last Xmas and would like to go again so much. I guess John B— and Charley Simpson are still single.

Ella, I have a very sore thumb, so I know you will appreciate my letter more. It is on the hand I use in writing. I took cold in a tiny sore. Do not have any idea how the sore was caused in the first place. I will close this time. Write to me soon. Don't treat Eddie badly when he comes to Washington.

Sincerely,
Your friend,

Orra

TO: *Miss E. L. Goode, 2508 M. St., N.W., Washington, D.C.*

Aldie, Va.
Nov 30, 1898

Dear Miss Lee,

Wednesday night again and just home from church and set down to write. I received your letter Monday evening as usual. Am more fortunate in getting my letters than you are as I have received every one from you the day after they were written. We are having winter weather up here. Last night it snowed real hard but the ground was so wet that it didn't stay any longer than morning. I received the Sunday World yesterday evening and amused myself last night looking at the pictures as it was so bad out that there was no preaching. Was up to Mr. Goode's Sunday night and went to church with Miss Maude. Everything looked quite natural and I found the way without a particle of trouble. I didn't go to Middleburg Thanksgiving night. It was right cold and I had a bad cold so I thought I had better not go out in the night air but if you had been here I am quite sure I would have gone anyhow. I believe I told you in my last letter that I didn't like the preacher that is holding the meeting here and I don't like him as well as I might yet but think he is a real good old man and I am trying to learn to like him. I don't know how long the meeting is going to last as he has said nothing about closing it yet. The congregations have been small every night and so far no large results are seen.

Oh! how about breaking that hat box when you had the fall. I understand you took it awfully hard but didn't care anything about breaking the lamp. Now of course I expect you will think Miss Maude told me about that too. I suppose you have heard from Miss Jordan before this and she has told you all the news. She told me last week that she had a letter from you and she told me lots that you had said. I told her she was right good at letting them I guess you know what. Among other things she told me that you had moved and you may imagine how surprised I seemed to be to hear that. John hasn't been down to call on her this week as the old doctor is away from home and he can't leave the store. He put in a full day last Sunday though he was down three times just going home to his meals.

And you had been to the theatre and enjoyed it and didn't see any harm in it either. Well I guess there is not much harm in just going once in a while. The harm comes in when you get to liking it too well and go there when you have other things to attend to, and then after become so fond of going there is danger of getting into bad company. I hope you won't be offended at this as I certainly intend no offense and say this in all kindness and because I feel interested in you and care for you. You may think the theatre a very innocent place to go to at first but after you go a few times you will change your mind. Now I say again that I don't mean to offend you at all neither am I finding fault with you for going to the theatre for I have no right to object to you going anywhere you please. I am simply giving my ideas on the subject. And in regard to you writing on Sundays I can't see anything particularly wrong in that but if you think it is wrong why then I think you ought to take some other day.

I had expected to come down to the city next week but don't know now whether I can come or not as we are right busy just now and it will be so near Christmas by the next week that I think it very doubtful if I can come before Christmas but will come if I can, I suppose you will soon know for certain whether you are coming up or not. You must be sure and come if possible and if not possible come anyhow. Now I must not close without thanking you for the Sunday World as I enjoyed looking at the funny pictures very much and also the news though I haven't read very much yet.

Well it is ten minutes of eleven so I had better close for this time. Trusting to hear from you soon I am as ever your true friend.

J. W. Bodmer

TO: Miss Ella L. Goode, No 2508 M. St., N.W., Washington, D.C.

E. B. GOODE,
Blacksmith, Wagons Made to Order,
Dealer in
Hardware * and * Farm * Implements.

BATTLE FOR LIFE
THE RETAIL
MERCHANTS'

Aldie, Va.,

Aldie, Va.
Dec 4th, 1898

My dear Friend,

Tonight I will endeavor to answer your kind and most welcome and long looked for letter and was more than glad to hear from you and that you are getting along nicely and that you are with your Ma's Aunt and Cousin for it makes it pleasant for you. The meeting closed Thursday night with no success. The weather was bad a good many nights and the people didn't turn out well.

Miss Jordan is well. I guess I saw her at Church soon after I recd your letter and told her what you said and she said she was going to write to you. I heard she had heard from you. I have not been to see her since you left.

Well John has been up once so he won't forget the way by Xmas and Mr. Goode invited him up again so you see he is all right. It is very strange you knew the meeting was going to commence. I know John told you. HaHa. Well now you must write nice letters to him so he can laugh a little. We were very sorry to know Mrs. Davis's son had the fever. I know she is worried and uneasy. Do hope he will recover. I got a nice long letter from Sister Lizzie since you left. She was well and happy and sent her love to you and said she was afraid you would break Mr. Bodmer's heart or leave a big hole in it. I talked real nice about you to him when he was up so you see I am a good girl and will help you along but the next time you leave Aldie and go to the city I don't want you to fall down and break your Hat Box because John might cry.

Well the Doctor is well. He has been to Baltimore for his Xmas goods and so has Mr. Bansick. Both have returned now. Randolph is well and still says Cousin Lee. Mary has been quite sick, is getting better now. She had yellow jaundice. Dr came every day for over a week. She looks badly. Nellie is busy all the time talking about Santa Claus. She sleeps upstairs with me now. We have moved our room over the dining room now. It is so nice and warm. She will wake up in the night and begin talking. She and Mr. Bansick have great times together. She has fallen in love with him. You see she is just like Cousin Lee, falling in love with all the boys.

Well Lee, Mr. Goode is having another well bored right near the back steps. The men are here now. They could not do anything with the other well. Will be glad when they get done. It will be quite nice, won't have to go off the porch. We killed hogs last week. Eliza is all done now. Wish you were here to eat some of the nice sausage but never mind, you shall have some Xmas when you come! We heard from Mother last week. She was as well as usual. I expect she will come down Xmas, so you will get to see her. Miss Sophia Carter and Mrs. Carter asks of you. I was up there Friday eve taking Randolph with me. Mrs. Frank Bodmer's baby is almost as large as he is. Mrs. Millie Tylor has a fine son. I don't guess John told you that, did he, I almost forgot it. Miss Jane is still in the city but I don't know her no. Will ask Mrs. Palmer sometime and tell you. Annie and Mary were proud of their letters you wrote them and Mary is always writing to Cousin Lee. Annie has sent her letter to Santa Claus. It was a real nice little letter and awful polite to him. Well I know you are tired of reading this scribbling. All join me sending best love. Eliza says come Xmas and let us know in your next letter and don't put off writing so long. Good bye

Your true Friend

Maude Ellison

Eliza is going to have a Christmas tree for the children. Won't that be nice?

TO: *Miss Ella L. Goode, #2508 M. St., N.W., Washington, D.C.*

Merrifield, Va.
12/4/98

Dear Ella

I will try and answer your ever welcome letter I received several days ago.

This is certainly a terrible day and it being Sunday makes it seem worse. Well, Ella, I suppose you are all ready for Xmas. It will soon be here. The year has been so short it seems impossible that Xmas should be so close to hand. Where are you going to spend your Xmas? I would like very much to have you come out here and spend part of your time anyways.

I have not been to Mr. Jacobs for quite a while. I want to go down before Christmas for a few days. I don't know how they like their new mother but from what I hear they do not get along very well. I guess a stepmother is not a very desirable thing to have. I believe the typhoid fever is decreasing somewhat in the neighborhood now since the weather has turned cool.

I don't know what has become of cousin Sallie. Mamma wrote to her about three weeks ago and we have never heard from her since. I want to come to the city before Xmas if I can, and I will be around to see you if I stay long enough.

Charlie expected to have to close his school as he was having such small attendance, but the "Supt" told him to try it until Xmas

Margaret Clara Settle Goode

any way and then he would see about it. He is getting very much out of heart about it but I hope it will do better.

Well I will close for this time. Write real soon and come up.

Yours devotedly,

May R.

TO: *Miss E. L. Goode, 2508 M. St., N.W., Washington, D.C.*

Aldie, Va.
Dec 14th 1898

Dear Miss Lee,

I have just come home from the store and although it is rather late to commence writing a letter I don't want to disappoint you for I guess you will expect to hear from me tomorrow as that will be Thursday and if you are like I am you would be disappointed if you didn't. I know if I didn't receive a letter from you on Monday, I should be badly disappointed. I am feeling better tonight than I did a week ago as I haven't had anything to trouble me and my trouble about the lecture wasn't as bad as I expected it would be. Most everybody said that I did exactly right and that makes me feel easy about it.

I don't think you are to blame about going with the young man if he is married as you didn't know he was married and if that is all there is to it why I wouldn't let that trouble you. You were not to blame at all if you did go to church with him.

Last Sunday was a lonely day for me. There wasn't anything going on at all in the evening or night. Of course we had Sunday School in the morning at ten, and there was preaching in the Episcopal Church at eleven but after that there wasn't anything at all to go to and besides it seemed like everybody had left town. Several of the boys went to Middleburg to church and some of the others went to see their best girls. John Hensley and Miss Jordan went to Middleburg at night as soon as her friend from Upperville went home. I haven't seen Miss Jordan to have any talk with her for several days so she hasn't had an opportunity to tell me anything you said in your letter to her. I don't believe I have had any talk with her since last Sunday a week when I was over to call on her.

It didn't rain up here that night only a little shower after I was over there but it stopped again before I left. John Hensley had been down all the afternoon and some of the boys played a joke on him. They told him that the old doctor wanted him up to the drugstore and after he got home he couldn't get back any more as the river was all out of banks and he had to get Hugh Bruin to take him across horseback. He was right mad about it. I saw Eddie Watson last Sunday but he didn't say anything about going to Washington. He is working for Mr. Jake Watson on a barn and I guess he can't get off right now.

I suppose all the stores look gay about the city getting ready for Xmas. Up here it don't look like Xmas is so near. I guess it will be awfully dull Christmas but then it is always dull up here. It seems more like Sunday than Xmas as a general thing. But if you come up it won't seem so dull to me as it never seems dull when you are here. I have just been thinking about coming down to Washington and have come to the conclusion that I can't come before Xmas and that is so near now and you are not sure of coming up. I thought that if you didn't come why I would try and come down soon after Xmas. But you must come if you can possibly do so and if you will let me know what day you are coming I will meet you in Leesburg provided of course that none of Mr. Goode's folks are not going over that day.

It may be that they will have business in Leesburg and will go over the day you come up but if they don't it will be a real pleasure for me to meet you any day you say. Now don't say you won't come because I am coming down, for if you come up I won't go until along after Xmas. That will suit me just as well as I haven't any business in the city at all and whenever I come it will be just to see you. I do hope you can come for I think there are going to be several Xmas entertainments about at different places and we could go to them all. We are not going to have anything at our church but they are going to have some kind of an entertainment at the Episcopal Church and then we can go to Middleburg as I generally go up there. There is going to be an oyster supper at the hall next Tuesday. Wish you could be here but guess it is impossible for you to come. I shan't say a word about your troubles with the married man.

And now it is getting late and I will have to be up early in the morning as they are going to butcher here and want to get an early start so I will have to get up soon or not get any breakfast. Wishing to hear from you again real soon, I am as ever your sincere and true friend,

J. W. Bodmer

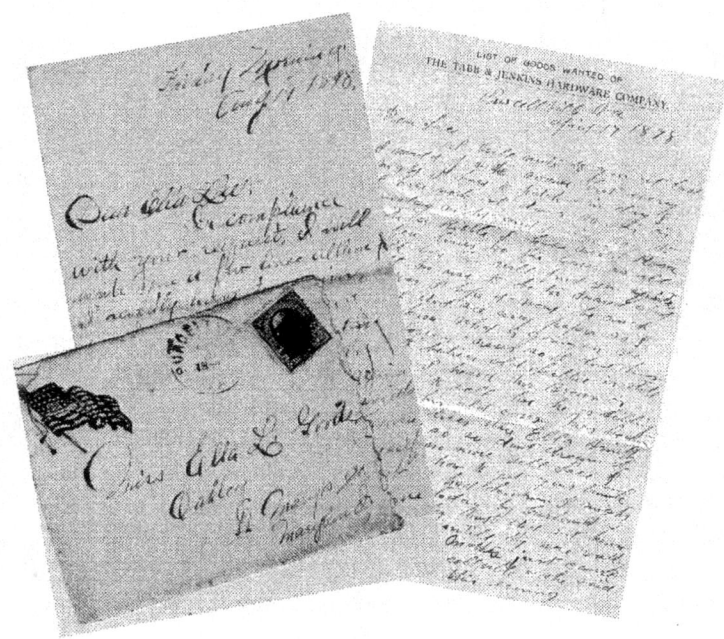

1899

Jan 1st, 1899
Aldie, Va.

My dear Friend:

Tonight I will endeavor to write you a few lines hoping you are quite well and happy that you have spent a merry Xmas and will enjoy a happy new year. We were disappointed you not being able to come up but Lee, come whenever you can and you know I will be glad to see you. I guess you have seen John ere this and he has told you all the news. I know you enjoyed hearing it. I think he was real selfish or he would of asked me to of went with him to see you for I want to see you as well as he does. I could of went to bed while you all talked. Now don't you think so? I told Mr. Vansickler what you said and he laughed and said tell you he guessed one out of Aldie was enough to come to see you. See he thought John would be enough. Lee, do you ever hear from Mr. Jenkins now? How has Mrs. Davis's son gotten? We have never heard from them. Do hope he is getting well again. Miss Sophia and Mrs. Carter are well. They always ask of Miss Lee. Sister Lizzie did not get off either, so noone here but mother.

This has been a quiet Xmas. Nothing much going on. I wish we could get together once more and have a nice little quiet chat and enjoy ourselves. We didn't have no good time together the last time you were here. Now when you write tell me all the news and a long letter. Take good care of yourself and don't forget your true friend

Maude Ellison

Ma sends her love to you. I just put my letter in Annie's. Poor child she surely has been ill and looks awfully bad now. We were real uneasy about her. When you write home give my love to them all and tell them I would love to see them.

Oh, Lee I must tell you, Tom gave me a nice little Xmas gift. Now don't you wish you were me. Miss Jordan went home today so they say will be back in about two months. I did not get down to see her before she left.

Dear Cousin Lee,

I will write you a few lines. How are you getting along now? I am sorry you could not come up Christmas. I was sick Christmas and not well yet. I got good many presents. Write to me some time. Aunt Lizzie could not get up Christmas. Grandma is with us now. We had a Christmas tree. We have not took it down yet. All are well. Willie and Mary has gone to a party tonight. I was not well enough to go. I would like to have gone. Mabel was up here at noon. Aunt Maude says write to her some time. I will not be able to go to school Monday. When are you coming up? It is getting bed time now. I will finish your letter tomorrow.

Papa and Mamma is making off bills now. Randolph is sick, he was sick all night. It is raining hard and I am sorry too. I was going out today. I hope you had a good Christmas. Mary and Willie is playing cards. I cannot eat anything. We have dug another well. We have a nice pump. It is easy to pump. All send love. Willie says write to him soon. Rachel and Mabel has bad colds now. I like to write letters. Mary is playing. It is getting dinner time now. We have a pretty play house. I will close your letter.

> Annie C. Goode
> Aldie, Va

No envelope

> Alexandria Va
> Jan 7th, 1899

Dear Miss Ella,

I am still in Alexandria and will not go home until Monday. When I got over here yesterday I found that Lewis had written home that he wouldn't come until Monday. I wasn't very badly disappointed as I will have another opportunity of calling on you before going home. You spoke about going away and staying all day Sunday so I thought I had better let you know that I hadn't gone home and I will come over Sunday some time. Will try and come soon enough to go to church if isn't too cold. But if I don't come in time and you want to go to church don't wait for me for if I don't come early I won't

> *Children of Edward Benjamin Goode and Eliza Ellison,*
> *resided in Aldie, Va.*
>
> ### (Eliza Ellison Goode 1860–1935)
>
> 1. Annie C.   b. 1889
> 2. Mary   b. 1890
> 3. William   b. 1893; d. 1932
> 4. Nellie   b. 1895
> 5. Randolph   b. 1898
> 6. Robert   b. 1899; d. 1959
>
> Dates from gravemarkers at Middleburg Memorial Cemetery and the
> 1900 U.S. Census. Census records also show Alice M(aude) Ellison,
> Eliza's sister, living with the Goodes at the time.

come until afternoon. I don't know what time you will get this but
hope you will get it all right. As ever, your sincere and true friend

J. W. B.

TO: *Miss E. L. Goode, 2508 M. St., N.W., Washington, D.C.*

Aldie, Va.
Jan. 15th, 1899

Dear Miss Ella,

I received your letter Friday evening. Guess it ought to have
come on Thursday as I noticed it was written Wednesday but I just
thought you forgot to mail it until Thursday and then it couldn't
come up until Friday. This is Sunday evening and I am feeling awfully lonely. I have been to preaching twice today, at the Presbyterian
Church this morning and at the Methodist this evening. I don't suppose you have been to church more than once today as it seems to be
a hard matter to get to church in the city. I was down two Sundays
and only went once and if it hadn't been for you I don't expect I
would have gone at all. I didn't go to Middleburg Saturday to
Quarterly meeting, the weather was too bad and the roads are just

awful. You just ought to see the streets of Aldie. The mud is about a foot deep. It's all you can do to get along uptown but not quite so bad down in our end of the town.

Don't you give people your address when you write to them? Miss Jordan says you don't. She sent up to me for your address. Said she wanted to write to you and didn't have your address. She didn't write to me though, she wrote to little Jennie Wrenn and asked her to get it from me. Jennie said that Miss Jordan wanted to come back to Aldie awfully bad as she had the blues ever since she left here. She must like Aldie. John seems lost since she has gone. We hardly ever see him in this end of the town now. I don't know how he is going to get along for the roads are too bad for him to go to Haymarket now.

Mr. Wrenn is going to change clerks Monday. Hugh Bruin is coming here and Mr. Ogden is going to Halfway in Hugh's place. They are just going to change places. That will suit Hugh better as he will be right at home. Miss Maude has gone away on a visit to her brother's at Halfway. I didn't get to see her before she went but I reckon she won't stay very long and I will go up to see her when she comes back. Mr. Goode hasn't asked me a word about you yet. I don't suppose he knows that I saw you at all while I was in the city. I haven't seen the old doctor yet but will deliver your message the first time I see him. I saw Eddie one day last week but didn't have any talk with him. He just passed by the shop and stopped long enough to ask how all the people in Washington were. I don't know who he meant but suppose he meant you. So I told him they were all well when I left. Lew and John Hensley are fixing to go to Middleburg tonight to preaching. I suppose it is so lonely for John here that he can't stand it to stay. And John Hensley isn't the only John that is lonely here for I have been lost ever since I came home. I haven't done much work since I came back but hope I will be more contented this week. If I went to the city very often I guess I wouldn't want to work at all as it takes about a week to get started again after I come back. There is lots of sickness up here. When I came home I couldn't hear of nothing but sickness and it seemed to me like everybody was sick and there are still a great many that have the grippe, although I am glad to say that none of our family have it and they are all well at Mr. Goode's. Well I must stop for a while as they are calling me to supper.

Now I will try to write a little more for I have finished my supper and haven't anything else to do and if I had I would finish writing

John W. Bodmer

first. How is Uncle George getting along? Has he been to call on Miss Seaton yet? Miss Jane Cridler was out to Sunday School this morning and she don't look a bit like she is going to die any ways soon. She said when she came home that she had come home to die but she says now she has changed her mind and thinks she will live a while longer. But she says she hopes she will never see Washington again. You must take good care of yourself or you might get the grippe and think you was going to die like Miss Jane thought. I believe I told you in my last letter that I was feeling perfectly well and that I guess I must have been homesick but I reckon I must have taken cold for the next day after I came home I felt awfully badly and it lasted for about three days. But I am feeling like myself again now. I suppose some people would have thought they had the grippe as that is what everybody calls a bad cold nowadays.

I suppose you are not thinking about coming up yet anyhow. I won't look for you until I see you but if you do come up here or go up to your home I hope you will let me know. And don't think for a minute that I don't want to see you or that I don't care anything for you for I had rather see you then anybody else and that's more than you can say about me I know. Well I reckon I had better stop for this time as I have written a lot now that won't interest you. So goodbye for this time. Write soon to your sincere friend.

John W. Bodmer

TO: Miss E. L. Goode, 2508 M. St., N.W., Washington, D.C.

Highland
(postmarked Haymarket)
Jan 17th 1899

My Dear Miss Goode,

Your dear sweet and interesting letter was received several days ago. I was glad to get it too for I enjoy reading your letters so much. You were very lucky to get such nice Xmas presents—the idea of a diamond ring. That must mean something. I suppose J. B. gave you that, did he not?

I got twenty presents but nothing quite as good as a diamond. I got a gold pen with pearl handle, a lovely ring set with pearls, a beautiful dark blue silk parasol that is handsome, a pair of kid gloves, and then most of the others were little fancy things. I had a grand time the last week I was in Aldie. Had nothing to do but go about and have a nice time. Was invited out to four Xmas dinners, of course J. H. was too. We went to several Xmas trees or entertainments. Yes I will tell you what J. B. got off the tree at the Episcopal Church. It was a bottle of water and a ginger cake. I don't know who put it on for him. He accused me of doing it but I did not. Some of the smart Boys put a monkey on a stick on the tree for me. I think J. B. had something to do with it.

I suppose you were delighted to see Mr. John B. and spent many sweet hours together. He was over home the Sunday night before I left Aldie. Well there were five young men there that night. Well the fun we did have or perhaps Lew or John told you about the way they teased John Moore. It was a shame. I have certainly missed the Boys since I left Aldie. But the only consolation is that I will go back again in the Spring. I will go to Baltimore about the middle of March for my spring stock. Wish you could go with me. Don't you think you can? Mr. Hensley is coming down Sunday. You know he brought me home, and who should be almost the first one to meet me, why Mr. Wilcher. But he did not stay very long and I was glad too as long as Mr. Hensley was there.

Miss Lee, you must excuse this scribbling and mistakes for the children are all around the table shaking me, will do better next time, for I know I can if I try. Write real soon to your loving friend

Lillie

TO: *Miss E. L. Goode, 2508 M. St., N.W., Washington, D.C.*

Aldie, Va.
January 27th, 1899

Dear Miss Lee,

I didn't think this morning that I would be able to write tonight. I have been feeling very badly for three days and today I stayed in bed nearly all day. I have a very bad cold but hope it will be better in the morning. There is still a great deal of sickness up here, mostly colds or grippe. I reckon I have the grippe but I just call it a bad cold.

Well Miss Jordan told you about the present I got at the Xmas entertainment. I expected she would tell you the first opportunity she had. Not that I cared at all for I just considered it a joke and intended to tell you about it myself some day. I didn't much think that she had anything to do with it but just accused her of it for fun. I didn't have anything to do with giving her the monkey either and don't know who did. I suppose she is not going to Washington until she goes to Baltimore after her spring stock and it would be a real nice trip for you to go with her and help her to pick out her hats and bonnets. I guess she has missed the Aldie boys a great deal since she left here for there were some of them there nearly every night. John Hensley didn't go down to Haymarket last Sunday but he did go to Middleburg and he was talking about going up again tonight to an entertainment and oyster supper but I don't know whether he went or not.

I went up to call on Miss Maude last Sunday night and told her you was well and getting along all right when I was down to the city. She wanted to know if you sent any word to her and I couldn't remember whether you had or not. Somebody told me that she wanted to see you as she didn't have a chance to see you last fall when you were here. I thought she saw you every day but from what she says you must have slept all day or gone visiting. Hope she will see you next time you come up. Tell Mrs. Imlay I should like very much to know the jokes she has on you.

Well I reckon I will have to close for this time as I am feeling very badly. Excuse this short letter and bad writing for I really don't feel well enough to write. You must write me a nice long letter for I can read even if I am not well enough to write. Goodbye from your true friend,

John

January 27, 1899
37 S. St., N.W.

My Dear Miss Good,

I am very sorry that I missed you and your cousin Wednesday night as I have been quite anxious to have you come and do some work for me. Mrs. O'Reilley told me that you have a machine. Are you using it where you are working or will your cousin be able to bring it with her for use here? You know I have no machine at all.

I intended coming up to Mrs. O'Reilley's to spend last evening and to try and see your cousin but I was the victim of a very bad nervous headache and could not come. I shall be very glad to have your cousin come on Monday morning if she can do so and in the mean time I should like to hear from or see you as to terms, etc., and the machine. Would it be too much to ask you to come out tomorrow evening or sometime on Sunday? It will be impossible for me to get up there. Is your cousin (I do not know her name) staying with you or would she like to stay out here altogether while she is sewing for me? You will oblige me very much if you can come out tomorrow evening as I have to leave here at 8 o'clock in the morning to get to my work in time, so would be unable to see her if she waited to come on Monday

Very respectfully,

Leulah Rothrock

I will be at home by five o'clock tomorrow afternoon, so if your cousin could come early and be here by then she could get back home before the cars stop.

Aldie, Va.
Feb 1st, 1899

Dear Miss Lee,

I received your very nice and much appreciated letter Monday evening and was real glad to hear from you and especially glad that you wrote so soon as you did for I put off writing so long last week I was afraid that maybe you would do the same. But you see I am writing earlier this week and I guess you will be surprised to get a letter so soon. I am feeling much better than I was last week but still have a cold. Think I will soon be well of it though. I have worked every day this week so you may know that I am not very much sick. I only stayed in the house one day. That was last Friday though I didn't work on Saturday but was out to the shop most all day. Most everybody has gotten well here but Mrs. Goode. She has been sick for a few days, just a bad cold Mr. Goode says, but she is sick in bed.

John Hensley and Hugh Bruin went to Haymarket Sunday so I guess Miss Jordan was highly entertained, both of them there all day. They were both sick next day with colds and Hugh had to stay in the house until this morning.

I don't want to give you one of the photos that I have for they are not a bit good but when you come up if you want one of them I will give it to you then. It might get lost if I send it by mail and I shouldn't like that for some newspaper man might get a hold of it and copy it in the Sunday paper with the comic pictures. I am ever so much obliged for the Sunday World you sent me. I enjoyed it very much. We all were reading it and looking at the pictures last night and tonight. We are having winter time up here now and I guess in the city too. About six inches of snow and real cold, about as cold as it was New Years. I guess you remember how cold it was then in the house anyhow. How is the furnace doing now? It has just been a month since I came to call on you but it seems like it has been longer. When you get ready to come up don't wait for the roads to get good or you might have to wait until Spring. The road to Haymarket is as bad as any and John H. and Hugh said they got along all right. The road to Leesburg never gets very bad any time and I don't suppose the Purcellville road gets too bad to travel. So whenever you get ready to come just come on and don't bother about the roads.

We didn't have Sunday School last Sunday but I went to the Presbyterian Church in the morning. That was all the preaching there was that day. Everybody up here that have icehouses have been uneasy about not getting any ice but I guess they can all get their houses filled now if it stays cold another day or two. Mr. Goode is going to fill his tomorrow. Eddie Watson was up last Saturday. Said he didn't know when he was going to the city. Well, tomorrow is groundhog day and we will know whether winter is over or not. I think the groundhog will freeze if he comes out tomorrow.

I see in the paper this evening that there are three or four cases of smallpox in Washington and quite a good many cases in Alexandria so I guess it would be a little dangerous for anybody to go to Alexandria now, though I wouldn't be afraid of it myself. I am awful stupid tonight, can't think of a thing to write. I didn't know it was you told me about Miss Maude not having time to see you last fall when you were here. I thought someone else had told me. She never told me that you slept all day. I just said that in fun because she didn't have time to see you. I know you didn't spend much time visiting for you never came to see me a single time and I went to see you most every night. Well I guess I will have to close this dull letter for I don't know anything else to write. Trusting to hear from you soon and with best regards to Mr. and Mrs. Imlay I am ever your sincere friend

J. W. B.

TO: *Miss Ella L. Goode, 2508 M. Street N.W., Washington, D.C.*

Falls Church, Va.
Feb 2nd 1899

Dear Ella,

So you are still busy at your work, that is good, and we shall be pleased to have you come out and spend some Sunday with us Ruth has a cold but the rest of us are as well as usual. None of us have been in the city except just long enough to do buying. But Grandpa says he is going to see you as soon as the weather is good enough for him to go the city.

Ethel goes to the public school and stays all day so you see she does not have much spare time. Maurice comes in once in a while.

He has been staying at his grandmother's lately as his grandfather (Mr. Folin) died suddenly of heart trouble. He is still quite deaf and trying to get a pension. Both the Jacobs girls are married and both were married away from home. And as surprises—Lelia married Victor Schooley—I believe his name is. He carried the mail last summer while the camp was here. And Maggie a Frank Fields of Ballston. I understand Mrs. Jacobs has been at her mother's for some time for a certain event. But I do not know about that. But I have not seen her for a very long time.

Mrs. Maben is in Michigan as her father was ill. Mr. Maben and John are keeping house. I am sure the event has occurred at Mrs. Jim Taylor's but nobody says a word about it. Pearl Luttrill has been visiting her sister in New York most of the winter. Sarah has been in bed a long time. She is very weak indeed but we hope as the weather gets better she will be stronger.

Do you see Mrs. Fenwick now? I suppose she is wearing black again, she must miss her father so much. Tell me where the girls are. I never hear from them, whether they are at home or not, and is Rosa going to school any yet. Oh yes, and the Tews, I don't know anything of them—come out when you can

As ever—

Lillian R. Gordon

I have not had a bit of sewing done. Have done some myself and bought some things.

TO: *Miss E. L. Goode, 2508 M. St., N.W., Washington, D.C*

Aldie Va.
Feb 8th 1899

I received your interesting and most welcome letter Monday evening and it is now with pleasure that I will attempt to answer it. I have about gotten well of my cold and am feeling quite well. Hope you are well and that you haven't frozen yet for it is awfully cold up here and I suppose it must be as cold down there. There is about twelve inches of snow here and the sleighing is fine but it is too cold for me to go sleighing now. I went to Middleburg with Mr. Goode yesterday to a funeral and we went in a sleigh. Mr. Frank Green died

Sunday evening and was buried yesterday. I guess you knew him or at least you saw him when you were here. He died with consumption. His wife never came until after he was dead. Mr. Stanton was down and held the funeral services at the house.

Was very glad indeed that you have determined to lead a Christian life and hope you will join the church that you like best and the one you think you can do the most good by joining. I think that a matter that everybody ought to decide for themselves after taking time to think it over and make up your mind. Of course you know I would be glad if you would join the Southern Methodist church as I am a member of that church myself but if you like some other church better it would be better to join the one you like best. I don't think it would be best to put it off too long though and wait until you feel good enough to be in the church. You know that your sins are forgiven and that you are a child of God and you don't want to wait until you feel good enough to join church forever. Since I have been a member of church I have never felt that I was good enough to be in church and I have had old church member persons that everybody knew were Christians to tell me the same. Just trust in the Lord and read your Bible and believe that what He has promised He will surely do. And ask Him to keep you from falling into sin.

Well judging from the weather we are having I think the groundhog hit it right. You ought to be here now to enjoy the sleighing while it lasts—if you don't mind the cold. It is so seldom we have any sleighing here that everybody that has a sleigh has been making use of it ever since the snow fell. I suppose you have been at work this week or you would have gone home and I guess you never went home or I would have heard of it. It is really too bad that the young man that you mentioned in your last letter left as soon as you went down for he might have wanted to stay longer. I suppose you told Mrs. Henry Watson whether the young men that were at her house called to see you.

Am sorry you think me selfish with my photos but really the ones I have are not a bit good and I will have some taken the first opportunity I have and then you shall surely have one and as I said in my last letter if you come up soon I will give you one of the ones I have if you wish. Mrs. Goode is still sick but she is better than she was last week. So you think that if you are to have the smallpox you will have it anyhow. What is to be will be. You must be an old school Baptist. I can't believe that way. Wish I could for I want to go to Alexandria next month to conference but would be afraid of smallpox. There is so much of it there. I guess there will be a good many preachers that won't go. I saw Mr. Stanton Sunday and he said he didn't know whether he would go or not.

We have been busy working on sleighs for a day or two. Everybody wants to go sleighing. Guess there have been lots of them out in Washington. John Hensley took a young lady out sleighing last night and it snowed real hard. I told him he surely didn't think very much of her to take her out such a night as last night was. He is kept quite busy at the drugstore now, they have a graphophone and everybody comes in wants to hear it. I don't know if you can make out what that word is and I don't believe I could either if I hadn't written it. So I will write it again. Graphophone. That is a little better.

Well February is passing right fast and you haven't come up yet. You were going to spend the whole month here and at your home but if you don't look out the month will be gone before you know it. But I know you can't leave your work any time you would like to. You are something like I am in that respect. I can only go when other people don't want me to stay. That is when I am not busy in the shop. But I expect you will find an opportunity to leave the city for a while sometime soon. I hope so at least for it seems a long time since I was down there. If you would come up now anybody could go to station for you in a sleigh and the roads are fine.

Guess I will have to close as I am getting sleepy and don't know anything else to write. With kindest regards to all, Uncle George and Grandma included. I am as ever your sincere friend. Write soon.

J. W. B.

TO: Miss Ella L. Goode, 2508 M. St., N.W., City

The Victoria, Washington
February tenth

Dear Miss Goode,

I intended answering your note soon after receiving it, but I was so very busy and for the last few weeks have not been very well. I was sorry to hear you were not well at Christmas time. I trust you are all right and have had all the work you could do. I will not want any sewing done before sometime in April. Then I think I will have some ginghams made. How far ahead have you made engagements? You can let me know about your time and we can fix a date later.

Yours truly

Mrs. Geo. Christiancy

TO: *Miss E. L. Goode, 2508 M. St., N.W., Washington, D.C.*

Aldie Va.
Feb 26th 1899

Dear Miss Lee,

I guess I will have to stay in the house all the afternoon as it is raining right hard so will spend part of the time in writing. It seems as if it rains or snows every Sunday and it is so awfully dull on stormy Sundays. I went to Sunday School this morning and have been reading ever since I came home. Have just finished a book and feeling dull and sleepy. It is quite different from what it was last Sunday. Then you could hardly go anywhere on account of the snow and today there is hardly any snow in the roads but it is getting awfully muddy. There was to have been preaching in the Episcopal Church this evening but I guess the preacher won't come, it is raining so hard. It is too bad that it is stormy every Sunday. There hasn't been any preaching here this month.

I suppose you haven't taken the smallpox yet. People up here are getting scared up about it and are getting vaccinated. It was reported that there was a young man about eight miles below Aldie had it but I heard a day or two ago that he had the measles. He had been to Alexandria and I suppose that was the reason they thought he had smallpox.

Well we didn't get washed away but the river did get right high and at one time we were all getting uneasy. The ice commenced to lodge at the bridge and we thought that it would dam the water up and throw it out of banks but the ice soon broke away and the water soon run down. I was real sorry you were feeling so badly when you wrote your last letter. Hope you are all right again by this time. If you think it is caused by your eyes I would have them examined for the longer you let it go on the worse they will get and if you have to wear glasses you will be right in fashion. I think glasses would be very becoming to you and if they were not I would rather wear them than to ruin my eyes.

I don't know yet when conference is to be held. I heard it was to be in Staunton but don't know whether it is or not. If it is to be there I won't be able to go. There is some talk of holding it in Washington. Hope they will have it there. Then we could all go. I suppose you will be gone home now soon, as the roads are getting so people can get about again and after you stay up there a while the roads will be so you can come down here. But I don't expect you want to come here very bad. I wonder what has become of Miss Jordan. I don't think Mr. Wrenn has heard from her lately as he generally tells me whenever he has a letter from her. I guess John knows where she is and I think I will ask him next time I see him. I don't expect he can go to Middleburg today, it is raining so hard. Mr. Ogden went down in Fairfax this morning to see his friend for the first time since the first of January. He has farther to go now and so he can't go so often. Tell Mrs. Imlay that this would be a good time to take the trip up here as the mosquitoes and the little harvesters wouldn't trouble her and I'll leave the shop unlocked and tie the dog.

I saw Miss Maude this morning at Sunday School. She said they had a letter from George a few days ago. Said they came near being snowed under. So I guess there was as much snow at other places as there was here. I think you might tell Miss Nettie about the young man from Falls Church. Hope you are not having such hard a time now as you were while the weather was so cold and I hope it will be warmer now at least in the morning so I can take this letter up to the post office.

And now I guess I will close trusting to hear from you soon and you needn't be afraid of writing too much for I enjoy your letters very much. Your sincere friend,

J. W. B.

Aldie Va.
Mar 1st 1899

I received your letter this evening and will answer it right away. I don't know why I didn't get it yesterday. I suppose though that Mrs. Palmer overlooked it for I see by the postmark that it came to Aldie yesterday. I guess you won't get this before Friday as I don't think the mail from here gets to Leesburg until after morning train goes up. I would be very glad indeed to come up Sunday if I knew that the roads were so that I could get there in a buggy but the last time I heard anything about the roads up that way there was still too much snow to get along anyway except horseback and I wouldn't like to undertake to go so far horseback If you hear whether the roads are so I can get there in a buggy you can let me know Saturday and if possible I will come up anyhow Sunday. Am sorry you have such a short time to stay for if I can't come next Sunday I know it would be so that I could come Sunday a week. I just heard today that Miss Jordan was coming up here next Sunday week so if she comes next Sunday John H. will be surprised to see her as he is the one who told me she was coming Sunday after next. Have you written to Miss Maude that you were going home? If you haven't maybe I had better tell her, you can let me know when you write. Mrs. Goode is still sick. She had been better but Mr. Goode said today that she wasn't very well. Yes I have heard that they were to hold conference in Washington and hope it will be so that I can attend but I know I can't go down Easter and stay. Guess I can just go and stay for two or three days. I hope you will be able to come to Aldie if I can't come to Purcellville but I am surely coming if I can.

Excuse this short and badly written letter for I have written in a hurry. Trusting to see you soon and also to hear from you sooner. I am as ever your sincere friend

J. W. B.

1413 V Street
March 11th, 99

My dear Miss Goode:

We will be glad to have you for a week just as soon as it is possible for you to come. Will you let us know a couple of days beforehand so that we can have everything ready?

Yours truly,

Eleanor D. Ogden

Aldie Va
March 16th 1899

Dear Miss Lee

I received your very nice and much appreciated letter Monday evening and was glad indeed to hear from you. I had begun thinking that something had happened to you or that you were sick but am glad to know that you got back to the city all safe and that you didn't meet with any accidents on the street. I guess you had a very quiet time while you were up home as you couldn't go anywhere and there couldn't anybody from any distance come to see you. I surely was disappointed that I couldn't come up for I had fully intended to come but I didn't have any idea how bad the roads were until I received your letter and then I inquired of people up near Philomont and they told me it would be impossible to get there in a vehicle.

Mr. Stanton came down to see us today. It was the first time he has been to Aldie for near two months. He is just over the grip. Guess he will preach Sunday. Miss Lizzie Ellison has gone back to New York. She only stayed from Saturday until Wednesday. She was to go home on Monday and did start to Leesburg but it was so cold and the snow commenced to drift in the road so Mr. Goode thought they had better not go so had to come back and stay until Wednesday. Hugh

Bruin, John Hensley and myself went up to call on her Sunday night. She is very pleasant. Miss Jordan came up last Sunday and stayed until Monday morning. She brought a young lady friend of hers along with her. Guess she enjoyed her visit for John H. was with her from the time she got here until late at night. She stayed at Mr. Bruin's as there was noone at home at Mr. Wrenn's. Mrs. Wrenn's mother died last Saturday and they were all down in Fairfax. I think Miss Jordan said she was going to Washington and Baltimore this week so I guess you will see her before she comes back here. It was too bad that you missed seeing George.

I appreciate the little picture very much and think it is real good. Tell Mrs. Imlay that I thought she would prefer staying in the shop but if she would rather come to the house why it will be all right for we don't let people spend the night in the shop very often and when we do it is only as a special honor to them.

I guess the Methodist people are making preparations for conference. I hope it will be so that I can come down and spend a few days but can't tell yet if I can come or not but will try and come if only for a day or two. Miss Maude told me Sunday she had a little box she would like for me to take to Washington if I went. Suppose it is for you as she laughed and said she has forgotten the address for it to be left. I guess that by the fifth of April there won't be much smallpox in the city so I don't think I would be running any risk of taking it.

I suppose you are wearing glasses by this time and if I should happen to meet you on the street I would hardly know you. Oh I forgot I must tell you what Miss Jordan said. She said that you had been up to see her Sunday before last, the Sunday you were at home and then she said that you were coming to see her last Tuesday and that she was going back to the city with you. Don't guess she expected me to believe what she said but she talked as if she was in dead earnest. I saw Eddie Watson today and he told me he was down to the city last week but only stayed a short while and didn't get to see any of his friends.

You must excuse this letter for I am right tired tonight and don't you wait so long this time as you did before but write real soon to your true friend

John W. Bodmer

89

March 21, 1899
Dynard Md.

Dear Lee

It is with much pleasure I now write you these few lines. I hope they will find you enjoying good health and having a good time and a plenty fellows. I am well myself but not having a good time at all, for everything is just as dull down here as can be. I haven't been to see a girl since I saw you last.

Geo. told me that you went over home not long ago. I would like very much to have gone with you. I suppose you had a nice time while you was gone. I heard you had joined Church and got good by nature as well as by name. I think I will join my Church and be a better boy. I have got the blues so bad I don't know what to do if I stay down here much longer. I am growing a year older every week of my life.

Have you seen the girls across the street lately? Give my love to them when you see them again. I have the promise of a place on a steamboat but will not know until first of April. I have a pretty good show for the place. But if I do not get it I will go away for good, better or worse I don't know which. I will be up to see you before I go away. I would been up before this but was afraid of the smallpox. It has been right bad up there I have been told. And haven't we had a terrible winter. It has been the worst I ever saw in my life. Is Rosa in Wash? I heard she was. Please tell me if she is and how long she is going to stay. If I get my place on that steamboat I will be in Washington twice a week.

Douglas has bought him a wheel. We had a race the other day. You ought to have seen us. Marion is going to move up with Geo.

Well this is all I have to say. I guess you will get tired reading this but I thought you could read it when you had nothing else to do. Goodbye with fond wishes

Bruce

Hoping to hear from you soon. Everybody around is well I believe.

Aldie Va.
March 23rd 1899

Dear Miss Lee,

I guess you will think I have waited a long time before answering your very much appreciated letter and to tell the truth about it I have put it off longer than I had intended but have been prevented by one thing and another from writing sooner. I thought sure I would write last night but went over to the store and the clock wasn't right so when I came home it was too late to begin writing. But I guess you think that the longer I put off writing the longer it will be before you have to write again.

I hope you will find it convenient to go up to your friend Miss Jones' wedding for I have heard you speak of her quite often but don't remember ever having seen her. The roads are very much improved from what they were when you were up home, at least they are about here. So if you do go up to Purcellville I guess you will have more company than you did when you were home before. Last Sunday surely was a disagreeable day, raining in the morning and in the evening. The wind blew so hard you could hardly go out but for all that we had preaching three times, morning and night at the Presbyterian church and in the afternoon at the Methodist Church. There were small congregations though each time.

I suppose Miss Jordan hasn't called to see you yet for John says she isn't coming to Washington until Saturday and then coming up to Leesburg Sunday. She will tell you all the news I guess when you do see her. No John wasn't the only one that called on her when she was here but he stayed so much longer than Lew and myself. Hugh asked us to come over so we just went over and stayed a short while. You had better come up with her Sunday and when you get to Leesburg telephone over and I will come over after you or if you get this Friday you will have time to write and let me know if you are coming. Mrs. Wrenn's mother lived at Centreville about 18 miles from here.

I hope the weather will be better by the time I come down but I think I will enjoy myself if the weather is bad. I guess I could bring your hat down all safe. Don't think there is any danger of my getting the box broken for I don't fall down very often.

So you really trust I wouldn't know you with your glasses on and if you should happen to meet me you had better take them off and then I guess I would recognize you all right. It's very strange that Mrs. Watson's brother never heard of Lee Goode before. I thought that was the name you went by at home.

I'm glad Uncle George has a girl but guess as soon as she finds out about him she will drop him. Poor fellow, he must have a right lonely time. It's a pity he and his wife can't make up but I reckon they never will. I suppose the little girls, I can't think of their names, are taking music lessons and next time I come down guess they won't be as backward about playing piano.

I am counting the days until conference and though it is so near I guess it will seem a long time to me. I am so anxious to come to the city. But I reckon the longer it is the better it will be so that the small-pox will be all died out. I don't think I would be afraid of that now though as I see by the papers that there is very little of it in Washington or Alexandria either now. I told Miss Maude she had better go down with me when I go but she said she didn't think she could go but would like very much to go. Well I guess I will close for this time. Trusting to hear from you soon I am as ever your sincere friend

J. W. B.

TO: Miss Ella Goode, 2508 M. Street, City

"The Victoria"
April 2nd 1899

Dear Miss Goode,

I am going away on the fifteenth to be gone 10 days or 2 weeks, so will have to put you off until a week later. I trust it will not make any difference to you. We are not taking our meals in the café any longer, and go out to our meals. Can you do as you did before, have your breakfast and dinner at home? Then I will give you luncheon.

Yours truly,
Mrs. G. Chrisciancy

TO: *Miss E. L. Goode, 2508 M. St., N.W., Washington, D.C.*

Aldie Va.
Apr 5th, 1899

Dear Miss Lee,

I just take the time and opportunity of writing you a very few lines to inform you that I expect to come to the city on Friday. So if nothing happens you may expect to see me Friday evening. I guess you think this a very short letter but I really haven't time to write any more as I am writing before breakfast. Will tell you the news when I see you. Your friend,

J. W. B.

TO: *Miss E. L. Goode, 2508 M. St., N. W., Washington, D.C.*

Aldie Va.
Apr 14th 1899

My Dear Miss Lee

I guess you will want to know whether I reached home safe so will try and write you a short letter to let you know I got here all right. My youngest brother met me at Leesburg. I didn't miss that eleven twenty train Tuesday night. I mean Wednesday night. It seems like I have lost a day somehow this week as I keep thinking that it was Wednesday I came home. I saw Miss Maude this morning. She wanted to know how all the people in Washington were and when you were coming up. Mr. Goode also wanted to know if you were coming up anyways soon. He wasn't as thoughtless about you this time as he was when I was down in January. He asked me all about you, if you were still boarding at the same place and how you are looking. I guess he thinks you are working too hard but I told him you was looking real well. Have only seen Miss Jordan to speak to her. I don't think there is any truth about her and Lew having a falling out for he was over to call on her last night and stayed quite a while. So if they had a falling out they have made up again. Lucy Barron is here. She came the day I went to Washington. I don't know how it was that Lew nor myself didn't see her in Leesburg.

I told Miss Maude I didn't know where to leave the hat box as she didn't tell me where to take it. She said she guessed it was all right just so I left it in Washington. I have been at work today and it didn't go very hard with me although I have been quite busy all day. Generally when I go away on a visit and stay away a few days I don't like to go to work when I come back but I didn't mind it a bit this time. Mr. Goode is talking about going to city next week to see Buffalo Bill's show but don't know yet whether he can go or not.

Everybody here is very glad that Mr. Stanton came back again. Guess he will preach here Sunday as it is his day here. I hope you haven't missed me as much as I have missed you for I have felt very lonely ever since I came home. Everything is so quiet and then when night comes I get to thinking about you and wish I was down there just for an hour or two. I do hope you can come up soon. But I won't insist on you coming until you have time to come. Don't guess it will be too much trouble for me to come to see you when you do come, but if it is I will just come anyhow for I don't mind a little trouble once in a while, especially that kind of trouble. You must excuse this writing for I am not used to writing on paper that is not lined and I can't keep straight lines. Goodbye. Write soon to your friend.

J. W. B.

Didn't see the redheaded girl any more.

Aldie, Va.
Apr 19th 1899

Dear Miss Lee

I received your very nice letter Monday evening and was glad indeed to hear from you so soon. So I am not going to wait as long as I generally do before answering it. I guess you will get this before Saturday evening. If you don't it won't be my fault for it is only Wednesday night and you ought to receive this tomorrow evening.

I guess you haven't seen anything of Mr. Goode this week. He couldn't come to city, has been too busy. I suppose you went to the show today. I would like very much to have been there myself as that is the only show I ever cared to see. I met Miss Jordan on the street last night as I was going uptown and she asked me what had become of you. I told her that you wanted to know what had become of her. She said you had treated her real mean in not answering her last letter, the one she wrote you while she was in Baltimore. I told her you did answer it but she said you had not or if you had you must have addressed it wrong as she never received it. She said she would have liked very much to have seen you but as she never heard from you she didn't like to come for she thought you wouldn't be at home when she called. She asked me when I was going to write to you and I thought I had just as well tell her so I told her I was going to write to you tonight and she said tell you to write to her as she had lost your address. She also said she would like very much to see you. So now you see you were mistaken in thinking she was mad with you. I didn't think you would mind me telling her that I was writing to you. She has been trying to find out for so long.

Well I suppose Rosie came over to see you Sunday and you gave her some of the candy. If she did I think she was lucky to get any of it as I would have thought you would have eaten it all before Sunday. Sunday was a very disagreeable day up here. It rained and snowed and hailed and blowed and at night it was real cold. Cold enough for me to wear an overcoat to go to church. Mr. Stanton preached in the afternoon but there wasn't many out to hear him as the weather was

Robert L. Bodmer

bad. We had Sunday School in the morning and Mr. Campbell preached at night. I have just come home from up to Mr. Douglass's. Went up there to a meeting we had about Christian Endeavor. Some of them want to change it and just call it Young Men's Prayer Meeting. I guess it will be just as well to change it as some of them object to the Christian Endeavor pledge and if we just call it Young Men's Prayer Meeting we won't have any pledge and maybe more would take part in it.

I am surprised at you sitting up so late listening to a Negro dance. Thought you would have been too sleepy for that. You would be so sleepy at nights when I was down there. I told Mr. Goode about seeing your cousin Gus and he said he didn't think he had ever seen her. So next time you see her tell her that he says he don't know her. John H. put in a full day Sunday, went to church in morning and in evening went to Little River to preaching down there and to church here again at night. He don't give any of the other boys a chance to go to see Miss Jordan at all. There has been another young lady from Haymarket visiting at Mr. Bruin's for about two weeks but she went home today. Don't think any of the boys called on her at all while she was here. I think the Miss Moore you spoke about joining church is Mr. Will Moore's sister as I saw her at Mount Vernon two or three times while I was down. She isn't very young if it is her. Well I guess

I must close as it is eleven o'clock and I don't know anything else to write. Write soon to your true friend.

J. W. B.

TO: *Miss E. L. Goode, 2508 M. St., N.W., Washington, D.C.*

Aldie Va
April 26th 1899

My Dear Friend

I received your very nice letter Monday evening and although I am feeling awfully tired I will write you a few lines in reply. The weather is right warm and the days are so long that when night comes I am always tired enough to sit down and rest. The country is beginning to look right pretty now. All the trees are getting green and fruit trees are beginning to bloom and the fields look so nice and green. Wish you could come up and spend a few days for I guess a little country air would be good for you. Thank you very much for your kind invitation to come down next month. Would like very much to come but guess it won't be so I can get off about that time as we are most always very busy at that time of the year.

I am surprised at you selling the blue waist as I thought they were all the go in Washington and you ought to try and keep up with the styles. I haven't seen Miss Jordan since receiving your letter but will tell her what you said the first time I have an opportunity. I didn't tell her your address because she didn't ask me for it.

The Miss Moore that you spoke of joining church has a brother here, Mr. Will Moore, lives at lower end of Aldie. I am not acquainted with her, just know her when I see her. Next time your cousin Gus wants to know what I think of her tell him I think she is just all right and would like to hear her sing that song again. Did I say we had changed the name of Christian Endeavor to Young Men's Prayer Meeting? If I did I made a mistake. It is Young People's Prayer Meeting. It wouldn't have done to call it Young Men's meeting for the ladies take as much interest in it as the young men. The young lady that was at Mr. Bruin's was a Miss Hulfish. Don't know that she is a special friend of Miss Jordan's but they seemed to be quite friendly while she was here. Yes I have called on Lucy Barron several times since she has been here. Was over there last night. I just treat her like a little girl. She is quite young, I guess about 17 or 18 but she don't like to be called a little girl.

I expect I will have to close as this pen is so bad I can hardly write at all with it but will have a better one the next time I write and will try and do better. Whenever you want to come up here if you will let me know I will be only too glad to meet you in Leesburg. With kindest regards to Rosy and Mr. and Mrs. Imlay and Uncle George and Grandma also. Remember me to the children and write soon to your friend

J. W. B.

TO: Miss E. L. Goode, 2805 M. St., N.W., Washington, D.C.

Aldie Va.
May 11th 1899

My Dear Friend

I guess you expected a letter from me this evening and I fully intended to write last night but I had so much other writing to do that when I got through it was too late and I was tired and sleepy so put it off until tonight. Was very sorry to hear you were feeling so badly and hope you are better by now. I am real glad to hear that you have such a pleasant place to work now for as you say it is not so pleasant at other places.

Mr. Stanton was down this afternoon. Came down to help us with our Children's day service which is to be the first Sunday in June. So you think I was making fun of your singing by asking you to come up and help with the singing. If you won't do that you can speak a little piece if you wouldn't think I am making fun of you again. But I don't guess you want to come up here any more. Guess it is too dull for you after being in the city all winter. I surely would love to come down to the Peace Jubilee but don't see any possible way of doing so, and besides, we have had plenty of rain now and it won't be necessary for me to come. Was sorry to hear that you think I stayed so long when I was down before but I thought you were getting tired of seeing me so often. Will know better next time and will stay over in Alexandria more and go to see the red haired girl. I don't think she will get tired of me so soon.

Miss Jordan didn't come to Sunday School last Sunday. She went away somewhere with John Sunday morning. I think they went to Little River to preaching and while they were gone her friend Charlie from Upperville came down. He waited until they came back and stayed until evening but I heard since that he wasn't coming back any more but don't know how true it is. He brought a whole buggy load of flowers with him. Lucy Barron is still here and I go over two or three nights in the week. It is so convenient, just next door you know. It don't seem to be a bit of trouble to go over there like it is to go to some other places that you know of.

There was a show in Middleburg last Tuesday but I didn't go to see it. Was too busy. A good many went from here but they said it wasn't much of a show. Mr. Goode was going to take the children but it was rainy and so he didn't go.

Miss Jane has left Aldie again. Think she has gone over near Leesburg with some old ladies. I had a nice trip last Monday. went down to Haymarket after some new buggies and coming back had to stop out of the storm. Will have to go again next week. So if you want to go driving in a new buggy you had better come up soon. Mr. Vansickler has a new buggy and I guess Miss Fannie Carrington will get lots of nice drives in it now as he is going with her quite regularly.

Well I suppose I will have to stop for this time as it is getting late and I have some other writing that has to be attended to tonight. Trusting to hear from you soon I am as ever your sincere friend

J. W. B.

TO: Miss E. L. Goode, 2508 M. St., N.W., Washington, D.C.

Aldie Va
May 17th 1899

My dear Friend,

As this is a rainy night I guess I will try and answer your very much appreciated letter which I received on Monday evening. You know it most always rains whenever I write to you or come to see you. I have just gotten home from the pasture field where I went with my brother Robert to take the calves. They got out of the field and came home about dark and Bob was afraid to go so far by himself so I went along with him for company. We had to hurry back for we thought it was going to rain before we got home, but it didn't so I went over to see Lucy Barron for a few minutes and then came home and commenced to write. I hadn't seen Lucy for several days. She has been up to Mr. Prisson's for a few days and just came home so I thought I had better go over to see her. She is going home the first of next week and I don't know how I will get along without her. She has been here so long and it is so convenient to go over and talk to her at nights. You see it is really no trouble at all for me to go over there as I don't have to dress up and the other places that you spoke of I wouldn't think of going unless I did dress up a little.

Was glad to hear that you were feeling better and hope you are quite well by this time but a cold is much worse at this time of year than in the winter. The storm last Monday week wasn't very bad here, only a few small hail and they didn't do any damage. I haven't taken Lucy Barron driving since she has been here but she asked me tonight when I was going to take her. I told her not until it stopped raining. I want to go up to Middleburg next Sunday as it is Children's day up there. If you come up I will take you along with me and let somebody else take Lucy.

Yes Mr. Vansickler does go with Miss Carrington quite regularly. They went driving last Sunday. I guess he has cut the old doctor out entirely and it seems as if Hugh Bruin is about to cut John out. Last Sunday he went to church with Miss Jordan in the morning and in the afternoon he took her out driving and then to prayer meeting with her at night. John didn't like it very much and the boys teased him a good deal about Hugh getting ahead of him.

I am real sorry I can't come down to the peace jubilee next week but hope you will enjoy it. I think Mr. Vansickler is going just one day and Miss Millie Everett and Miss Blanche Carruthers are going. Guess they will stay several days. Tell Rosa that when she goes home she had better come by way of Aldie and stay a few days. We are getting ready for our Children's day service but we have so few scholars I guess we won't have as good a service as we would like to have. We meet twice a week to practice the singing and recitations. I expect they will have a very nice service at Middleburg next Sunday as they have a large Sunday School. Tell Ethel I will come over to see her as soon as I can. I guess I will have to close for this time as I don't know anything else to write and it is ten o'clock and I am beginning to get sleepy. With kindest regards to all the people and trusting to hear from you soon I am as ever your sincere friend

John

TO: *Miss Ella Goode, 2508 M. Street, City*

The Victoria, Washington
May 21st

Dear Miss Goode:

I will be ready for you any day, come as soon as you can. I have five dresses for you to make. Can you give me more than a week if I need you? You can tell me when you come.

Yours truly

Mrs. Christiancy

TO: *Miss Ella L. Goode, 2508 M. St., N.W., Washington, D.C.*

Ellicott City Md.
May 21st 99

Dear Lee

I will try to scribble you a note at least, I am not in much of a writing mood.

I have just written to my two Best Boys so that has taken nearly all my ambition. I went to church this morning, it being Whitsunday. It was a very nice walk. The country is lovely now. How much I would love to see the mountains and valleys of Loudoun Co just now.

How is your ma and how is Perry? Has he gotten better? Has Rosa gone home or is she yet in Washington? I am sorry I did not get over to see her before I left. Well for the Jubilee I suppose your country gent J. B. will come down for the occasion.

❧ 101

How is my dear little Maurice? I am longing to see him once more. I am tired to death and last night I let my glasses fall and broke one of the glasses in half. So I can hardly get along without them. I will send them to Wash and have a new glass put in. Hoping to have them returned to me in a few days. I am very busy. I have been working in the evening since I have been out here. I hope to return by June 15th or near that time. I have no news for there is nothing out here to write about. The grounds are beautiful and the flowers are coming out. So I will hope to hear from you soon.

With love to you I remain your cousin

Nettie

Write me all the news. You know how lonely it is out here. I am using the envelope I addressed last fall when out here. I will endeavor to get it off this time. I had a very nice letter from Miss Carrie Dellinger a few days ago. Love to Rosa.

TO: Miss E. L. Goode, 2508 M. St., N.W., Washington, D.C.

Aldie Va.
June 1st 1899

My Dear Friend

Well this is Thursday night and as I haven't heard from you I guess you won't come up Saturday for you know you said if you were coming you would let me know by Thursday. Am sorry you can't come this week as next Sunday is our Children's day and I would like for you to be here to say your little piece. I guess though you are something like I am and can't always leave when you would like to. I wanted to go to the jubilee awful bad but couldn't spare the time to go. The people that went from here don't seem to think much of it only the fireworks they say were real good. There is a strawberry festival going on here at the Episcopal Church but I didn't go. It was so rainy all the evening and I thought it was going to keep on raining so didn't make any preparations to go and after it stopped raining it was so late I concluded that I wouldn't go. They are having it in the church it is so wet and muddy outside. There is going to be another one here next week Friday and I guess I will wait and go to that.

It would be real nice if you could come up on Friday instead of Saturday and it would be only one day more for you to be away from your work. I saw Miss Maude yesterday up to church when we were practicing for Children's day but I don't know what is the reason she hasn't written to you unless it has been too warm for her to write for it surely has been awfully warm all this week. Little Randolph Goode was right sick for a day or two the first of the week but think he is all right again. I didn't go to Middleburg last Sunday but I did go on Saturday. Dr. Boyd preached a very fine sermon. Mr. Goode went up to hear him Sunday morning but I thought I had better stay to Sunday School Sunday morning. Hugh and Miss Jordan went to Haymarket last Sunday and John went away somewhere and stayed all day. I don't know where he went. Miss Jane Cridler has come back home again. It seems as if she can't stay away from Aldie very long at a time.

When you write let me know what train you are coming up on. There is one gets to Leesburg about eleven o'clock and another one about three o'clock in the afternoon. Come Friday if you can and if you have your new dress finished by that time. Trusting to hear from you soon and also to see you I am as ever your friend

John

TO: *Miss E. L. Goode, 2508 M. St., N.W., Washington, D.C.*

Aldie Va
June 10th 1899

My Dear Friend

I received your most welcome letter on Wednesday and was very glad to know that you had gotten home all safe but guess you had quite a lonely time of it. Mr. Goode was telling me yesterday that the train that you were on ran off the track and last night Miss Maude was telling me about it. I told her that I had seen something about it in the paper.

There was a festival here again last night and it rained as usual. It seems to rain every time there is anything like that here. But I had a very pleasant time if it did rain. It was in the school house and there wasn't a very large crowd. I liked that because it wasn't so crowded. Well it isn't quite so warm this morning but it surely has been terrible warm since you have been gone. The thermometer has been 100 for three days but it is raining now and maybe it won't be quite so warm. I haven't taken that trip to Haymarket yet. Won't go now until one day next week.

The girls from Alexandria are not coming up this week, at least we haven't heard anything from them. Guess they are going to wait a while. I am writing on Saturday morning as it was so late when I came home from the festival. You said it was Children's day next Sunday and that Rosa was to take part. Is it at Mount Vernon church? Guess it will be real nice and wish I could come down myself. Tell Rosa that she must not get excited. I suppose though that you will go to Alexandria. If you do and if you see anything of either one of those girls, the red headed one or the other one either you can just tell them that you saw me.

The wedding took place last Wednesday and there was quite a large crowd at church to see them married. The other bride that is to be named next Wednesday was at the festival last night. I will have to close for this time as I must go to work. Trusting to hear from you real soon I am as ever your true friend

John

TO: *Miss E. L. Goode, 2508 M. St., N.W., Washington, D.C.*

Aldie Va

June 15th 1899

My dear Miss Lee

I guess you think I am slow about writing this week but the weather is so warm I have been waiting for it to get a little cooler. I guess it is very warm in the city now for it always seems warmer down there than it does here. I took my trip to Haymarket last Monday and got caught in the rain as usual but that was no more than I expected as it was real cloudy in the morning when I started. But I needed the buggies and thought I had just as well go after them even if I did get caught in the rain for I am used to going in the rain you know.

There were a good many people from here went to the Upperville horse show today but I thought it was too warm to go that far to a horse show. Hugh and Miss Jordan went and Mr. Vansickler and Miss Fannie Carrington. Mr. Goode was going but it was so warm this morning he changed his mind and stayed at home. I think all the children at Mr. Goode's are well again. I saw Eddie last Sunday and told him you had been inquiring after him and don't you think he was in Aldie the Sunday you were here and then never came to see you.

Miss Leith was married yesterday but I didn't go to the wedding, it would have been too much trouble you know. We have a Washington young lady in Aldie stopping at Mr. Watson's. I would tell you her name but don't know how to spell it. It is Julyn but I don't think that is the way she spells her name. The girls from Alexandria that were to have come up to our house have not come yet and we haven't heard a word from them since you were here, guess they have gotten out of notion of coming. I suppose you will soon leave Washington now for the summer. Suppose Rosy is still in city. I guess I will have to stop writing for the bugs are about to eat me up but before I close I must tell you about Mr. Frank Jackson. He has really got a sweetheart and she is at his house on a visit this week. She lives in Leesburg and came over with him last Sunday. Now I will close. Goodbye, write soon to your friend

J. W. B.

TO: *Miss E. L. Goode, 2905 N. St., N.W., Washington, D.C.*

Aldie Va
June 23rd 1899
Friday Night

My Dear Friend

I received your very much appreciated letter Wednesday evening and although I am not feeling very well I will try and write you a short letter in reply. I have had a very bad headache all the afternoon and that is something I am not used to having and so it is worse when I do have it, or at least it seems so to me. I hope it will be better by morning as I want to go to Leesburg tomorrow. I have a new wagon over there and want to go after it.

I was surprised to hear that you had moved. Had no idea that they were thinking of moving but then I guess people in city move most any time. Sorry you don't like where you are but maybe you will like it better after you have been there for a while. I suppose now that Rosa has a place she will stay in city all summer. I rather guess she likes the city anyhow.

The young lady is still at Mr. Watson's but think she is going home tomorrow or Sunday. Mrs. Watson's youngest sister (Hattie) has been here too for about a month. I don't know of any more weddings up here now but if I should happen to get married will let you know in time so you can come to the wedding. John never comes down to call on Miss Jordan any more. Guess Hugh has run him off entirely. We had a letter from the Alexandria girls a few days ago and they expect to come up next week. I suppose you haven't been to Alexandria yet. Miss Fannie Carrington went home this morning and I don't know what Mr. Vansickler will do now. I guess he will be quite lonely for a while any way. I am sorry she has gone myself as we will miss her at prayer meeting and preaching for you know she always played the organ.

Well we have to go to church early in the morning now during the summer. Mr. Stanton is going to preach at 9 o'clock in the morning. Last Sunday he came down here before he had his breakfast. Overslept himself and didn't have time to eat before he came. He has gone away on a visit now for a few days. Gone to see his father's mother. I think they are all well at Mr. Goode's unless some of the children are sick and it seems like some of them are always sick. Miss Maude went to a lawn party yesterday evening down to Mr. Carruther's.

Well I guess you will be home by Bush meeting time and if I don't see you before then I guess I will see you up there. I asked Eddie the other day if he was going to Bush meeting and he said he didn't think he would, but I expect he will when the time comes. Goodbye for this time. Write soon to your sincere friend

J. W. B.

Aldie Va

July 12th 1899

My Dear Friend

I received your most welcome letter Monday evening and was real glad to hear from you but a little disappointed again that you are not going home until next week. But of course it is all right if you stay in the City all the Summer. By the time you get home now it will be so near Bush meeting time that it will hardly be any use for me to come up until then. I believe it begins the first day of August. Tell Rosa that I will have a real nice fellow for her when she comes to Aldie. Have been looking around for one since I received her message and think it won't be any trouble to find one and maybe I can find two or three for her and then she can take her choice.

Hugh and Miss Jordan have gone somewhere tonight. Don't know if they have just gone for a drive or whether they have gone to Middleburg as there is an entertainment up there tonight. I suppose you have had a letter from Miss Maude or Mrs. Goode since you wrote last as they sent down for your address a few days ago.

Last Sunday was quite a big day here at the Episcopal Church. They had a choir from Georgetown to do the singing, about twenty four boys most of them little fellows. I guess it was right nice but I didn't hear much of it. There was such a crowd that all the people couldn't get in church so I stayed outside. The choir marched into the church singing and after services were over they marched out again. They are boarding at Middleburg at the hotel.

I suppose you have heard that Mr. Goode has bought the blacksmith shop from Mr. Bruin. I didn't go to church with Miss Jane and Miss Maude last Sunday night. The meeting was at the Methodist church so Miss Jane didn't need to have anybody to go with her. I guess when you come to Aldie you will have somebody to go with you if I do have to go with Miss Jane. If you were here now you couldn't get to church in the morning for you know preaching is at nine o'clock and that would be too early for you as you can't get to church in city by eleven. We have to go at nine every Sunday for when there is not preaching we have Sunday School at nine.

Well I guess I had better stop as it is after ten o'clock. I didn't hardly expect to write to you tonight but had some other writing to do and after I got started thought I had just as well write tonight as to put it off until tomorrow. Goodbye for this time. Write soon to your true friend

J. W. B.

TO: Miss E. L. Goode, Purcellville, Loudoun County, Va.

Aldie Va
July 30th 99

My Dear Friend

This is Sunday afternoon and I have plenty of leisure time so will write you a short letter to let you know that I haven't forgotten you. I received your letter Friday evening. Am very sorry you can't be at Bush meeting on Wednesday. Guess I will go as I have made arrangements to go that day. You had better try and get there some way if you possibly can. If I knew just where you live and was sure you would go I could come up after you but I don't know exactly where you live and besides I might come after you and then maybe you would not care to go. I think I can stay two days and if you are not on the grounds Wednesday I will try and find my way out to your home Wednesday evening. I don't know if Miss Maude will go Wednesday or not. She is not at all well, has been sick since Friday night but is a little better today. Mr. Goode wants to go and if he goes she will go with him if she is well enough. Guess I will go alone as everybody else from here want to come back the same day they go.

Well it isn't necessary for me to write any more for I hope to see you soon and then I can tell you all the news better than I could write it. Guess you won't have time to write again before Wednesday. From your sincere friend

J. W. B.

Aldie Va
Aug. 31st 1899

My Dear Lee,

I hardly have time to write to you tonight I have so much other writing to do, but will take time enough to write you a short letter and you know that I most always do write short ones. Well this is the second night since you have been gone and I hardly know what to do with myself. It seems so strange for me not to go up to Mr. Goode's. Guess they miss us of nights—but reckon they won't get lonely for Miss Jane is there. Guess she and Gene will have great times now. I have missed you very much since you have been gone but have been quite busy and have gotten along better than I expected I would. Mr. Furr was down this morning and said that there was a very pretty young lady that he used to throw horse shoes at passed by his house yesterday and the harness broke and he said he told her that if anybody had thrown a horse shoe at her the harness wouldn't have broken. I heard that the harness broke the same morning you went home and I told Frank that I expected Mr. Furr would have something fixed up about it. I think Miss Lillie is going to move tomorrow.

I won't write any more this time as I am right tired and it has been such a short time since I saw you, I don't know anything to write. With kindest regards to all I am as ever

John

Write soon if you have not already written.

Aldie Va
Sept 12th 1899

My Dear Lee

I got home all safe Sunday night about half past eight. Could have gotten here sooner but drove slow after I got to Mountsville. It

Olive and Welby Seaton, two of Blanche and Clarence's children

took me just seventeen minutes to go from your gate to Purcellville and if I had driven as fast all the way I would soon have gotten here but was not in much of a hurry to get home so came along quietly. I came by Mrs. Silcott's and met Clayton this side of his home going towards home.

I told Mr. Goode about the wedding and he thought it very strange for a young girl like Blanche (I mean Mrs. Seaton) to get married but said he guessed it would not have done any good for your mother to have objected. I also told him what you said about writing to you about going to Maryland and he said he didn't know when he could go if at all if he keeps as busy as he has been the last few weeks. They are working in the new shop but are not done moving yet. Have not seen Miss Maude since I came home and guess I won't see her before Sunday. Mr. Goode brought Doris Ellison home with him last Sunday. He took Mrs. Ellison home and brought Doris back with him. Guess she will stay a while. Miss Jane came home yesterday. I don't know whether she has come to stay or if she is going back again. Miss Lillie did not come up with Hugh Sunday. Guess he was quite late coming home Sunday night as he didn't start from here until after twelve o'clock. He says he thinks she is coming up about the last of this week. I suppose there hasn't anybody else gone to Hamilton since Sunday. Hope you will let me know when you get ready to go for I would like to go with you.

Mr. Wrenn has company from Alexandria, a lady and her son. I'm not sure but think Lucy is coming up again soon. She told Lewis when she went home that she expected to come up again this fall and this evening Mrs. Moore passed by the shop and told me she had a message for me again. Said she would tell me what it was when she came back but I never saw her anymore so don't know what the message is but just think it is from Lucy and maybe she is coming up again. The other time she was up she told Mrs. Moore to tell me to come to Leesburg after her but I went to Purcellville instead of Leesburg. Guess I will do the same way this time if I have the opportunity but reckon I had better not go to Purcellville too often for some of you might get tired of seeing me so much. I haven't been to call on Miss Jane but think Gene is there tonight. Miss Jane's friend the professor has been in Middleburg for two or three weeks boarding at the hotel and a few days ago he went away and didn't pay his board bill and livery bill.

We are going to have rock pavements in our end of town too. They are hauling the rock today. Henry Watson has gotten a great deal worse again, guess he has typhoid fever sure enough and it will go hard with him as he is so fleshy. Well I am getting a little sleepy and besides I don't know anything else to write so will close. Trusting to hear from you soon and with kindest regards to all I am as ever

John

No envelope

Aldie Va
Sept 17th 1899

My Dearest Lee

I received your nice sweet letter yesterday evening. Expected it sooner but suppose you were too busy to write any sooner. I was real glad to know that you are enjoying yourself and should have liked to have been at the picnic myself.

I guess you will be surprised at what I am going to tell you now but it is not my fault and it may be that it will turn out all right, at least I hope so. It is about the meeting. It is to begin tomorrow night. I never knew a word about it until yesterday (Saturday) morning. I got a postal from Mr. Stanton to know what we all thought about beginning the meeting tonight. He had been holding a meeting at Landmark and closed it Friday night so he thought if it suited everybody here he would begin here tonight and as most everybody seemed to think it a very good time for the meeting he decided to begin tomorrow night. He would have preached tonight but it is Mr. Campbell's day here and he is going to preach tonight so Mr. Stanton will begin tomorrow night. I don't know how I can bear to go by myself but suppose I will have to for a few nights. I was thinking that maybe the best way for you to come down would be to come to Leesburg and I will meet you there. I don't guess the fare is very much from Purcellville to Leesburg and it would be so much more convenient for me to come to Leesburg than it would be to go all the way to your house. So if you can come to Leesburg just let me know what day you can come and I will be there to meet you. I suppose you will come on the noon train. It is much too far to go to your home and back here the same day and I am so busy. I don't like to lose any more time than I can help. Try and come Wednesday if you get this in time to let me know. If not come any day it suits you to come. You had better write to Miss Maude when you are coming so they will know.

Miss Lillie was here last Friday, came up in the morning and went back same evening. Hugh says he don't like the idea of going to church by himself either. It is getting dark so will close and will tell you all the news I know when I see you. Write right away now and let me know what day to meet you in Leesburg.

John

P.S. Since writing this I saw Miss Maude and we were talking about you coming down and she said she would write to you and tell you about the meeting and I told her to tell you to come to Leesburg and I would meet you there. She said that they had been thinking that would be the best way for you to come. I never told her that I was going to write to you so I guess you will get two letters tomorrow. I have been to preaching three times today and Sunday School this morning. Hugh Bruin says this has been an awfully lonely day.

With love to all I am as ever

John

TO: *Miss E. L. Goode, Purcellville, Loudoun County, Va*

Aldie Va
Sept 19th 1899

My Dear Lee

I received your most welcome letter this evening and will answer it right away. Was glad to hear from you so soon but very badly disappointed to know that you can't come down this week for I was most sure you were coming when I got your letter so soon but was disappointed when I read it. I hope it will be so you can come soon. If you could come Saturday I would be very glad to meet you in Leesburg if it is so you can come. If you can't come Saturday but can come Sunday let me know and I will try and come up Saturday evening but if you can't come down with me I don't expect I ought to leave

Sunday School and it would be too late to start after Sunday School for I would want to be here at night to preaching. As you say if you don't come soon you won't have long to stay if you expect to go to the city the first part of next month.

Miss Lillie is going to Baltimore next Monday and then she is coming here the first Sunday in October. So if you come next Saturday or Sunday you will be here a week before she comes. The idea of you wanting to go to church with Hugh and let me go all alone. But then I have been telling you that you had rather go with some one else. I don't think though that Hugh would want to go with you if Miss Lillie was here. There wasn't any preaching tonight. It is so rainy. Has been raining all the afternoon and evening and is just pouring down now. Looks as if it might rain for a week but hope it won't for if it did it would break up the meeting.

I must tell you about the message Mrs. Moore said she had for me. You remember I told you she said she had a message for me and I thought it was about Lucy coming up again. Well it was poor Lucy. She only sent her love to me and said maybe she would come up some time this fall. Now wasn't that nice for her to send her love to me? She is about the only girl that ever sends her love to me. Hugh says he is still lonely but says he is going to Haymarket Sunday and then after that it will only be one week until Miss Lillie comes here to stay and then I will be the only one who will be lonely. But guess I will have to get used to being lonely. Now I will close trusting to hear from you right away. I am as ever yours

John

TO: *Miss Lee Goode, Purcellville, Loudoun Co., Va.*

Chantilly Va
Sep 19th 99

My Dearest Lee

Your nice letter came one week ago and not answered yet. It really looks too bad.

Do not think for a moment in my long silence I have forgotten you dear Lee. During the past week a Baptist revival has been going on right near us. I have been several nights. Indeed believe me I am becoming a right good Baptist, in plainer words no "not if I know myself." I think the minister a very good preacher but that is all. The Hurst girls nearly always stop in and want me to go with them is the reason I go as often as I do.

I do not know if I told you in my first letter or not about the coolness that came over the girls while I was up to Aldie. It seems John told the girls I refused to speak to him up to Camp Meeting and I never saw him at all. I said when I found out that was the trouble with the girls it certainly seemed fate was against me that day. Does it not look the same way to you? When I came home soon discovered there was something wrong with the girls and what it could be puzzled me to some extent until I found out from some others and they never mentioned such a thing to me.

Florence is now up the Country with her sister Mrs. Lang. Her husband has to be away so much is afraid to be left alone so much. Miss Jane spent last week with us. You remember she was anxious to come down to the cannery. Well she came. Her work was to be labeling the cans, in the mean time the labels gave out. While waiting for others to come Miss Jane grew very restless and wanted to go home so Papa took her home last Monday. He insisted on her spending more time with us but she seemed anxious to go home.

I expect Rob down next Saturday or Sunday. Sincerely hope nothing will happen to prevent him from coming as you know how hard a disappointment goes with me, my dear. I would love so much to be in Aldie when the meeting begins. But I expect to begin teaching next month. Why do you not come from Aldie down to see me on your way to the city? I think this would be just splendid, now why cannot you do this. Am sure you can if you will only think so.

We are having lovely nights now aren't we? I do enjoy the moonlight so very much or rather used to when Rob was not so far away.

And now my dear I must conclude my letter with lots of love. Write real soon.

Lovingly, Your true friend

Marguerite Mae

Two lovers are like two armies
Generally get along quietly together until they are engaged.

Aldie Va
Oct 17th 1899

My Dearest Lee

That is allright about my not coming up tonight. So I will stay home tonight but will come up tomorrow night. I won't go to see Miss Lillie tonight as you said she was expecting someone else but will see her sometime soon. Don't work too hard tonight and don't stay up too late either for you might be too tired and sleepy to see me tomorrow night. Excuse this writing as I haven't any more time to spare. Goodbye. Will see you tomorrow night
With love

John

Aldie Va
Oct 27th 1899
Friday Night

My Dearest Lee

I don't know a thing to write but as I kind of promised to write to you tonight I will try and keep my word. I got home all right about six o'clock. Would have gotten here sooner but stopped at Mr. Crouch's a while. Just got here in time for supper. I am always on hand at meal time. I stopped and left the package for Miss Maude. Didn't see anybody but Doris and Annie but guess they gave it to her. Haven't seen Miss Jane since I came home. Don't think she has been down town. I saw her letter in the Mirror and suppose you did too. She said that rumor said that one of Aldie's most dignified young men was to be married in the near future. There don't anybody much seem to know who she means and I won't guess I would know either if you hadn't told me about it Sunday.

I didn't have to go to Haymarket. Lew went for me the day I came home. I was very glad he did for I didn't fancy the trip very much. Miss Lillie went and took little Sadie Whitlock with her. Hugh couldn't get off to go with her.

There has been a death here since you left. Mr. Hogan. I guess you heard of his being sick. He had consumption and died Thursday morning. Is to be buried in Leesburg tomorrow. Henry Watson is coming up home tomorrow to stay a while. People down here want to know if I was up to the mountain to put the fire out. I tell them yes I went to help put it out.

I have felt very lonely all day today although I have been busy and ought not to have been. I stayed up until half past ten last night writing and have done a good deal tonight. Wanted to get through tonight so I wouldn't have any to do tomorrow night so I will have time to study my Sunday School lesson. Guess you will go to Sunday School if you don't go to Hughesville. I think Mr. Vansickler is going. Mr. Stanton was down this afternoon and I won't have to go to Unison after Dr. Boyd. He is going to bring him down himself.

Now you must write real soon for I miss you so much and if I can get letters from you it seems almost like seeing you for you write exactly like you talk. I guess I will come to Washington soon after you go there for I want to see you real badly now but know I can't go to see you very often after you do go there. Give my love to all at home and write real soon to your loving friend

John

TO: *Miss E. L. Goode, 39 S. St., N.W., Washington, D.C.*

Aldie Va
Nov 10th 1899

My Dearest Lee

I have been over to Mr. Wrenn's store and was thinking about you and thought that perhaps you were feeling lonely at your new home and that maybe a letter would cheer you up a little. So came home from the store and will write you a short letter anyhow. I didn't receive your letter until Thursday, guess I ought to have gotten it Wednesday as it was written Tuesday night. While I was at the entertainment here you were at home writing. I didn't think it was very good but guess it was because I had heard the same thing twice before. Miss Maude did not go. She stayed home with the children and let Mrs. Goode go. Miss Jane was there and she didn't come down to borrow the quarter from me either. Said she had two quarters. I kept door for them so got in free. Was more of a crowd there than I expected and took in about seventeen dollars.

Guess you have got settled down in the city by this time and are ready to go to work Monday. Seems to me you are in a strange part of the city. Don't think I was ever in that part of town and don't know whether I could find you if I was to come to the city now.

We haven't had any prayer meeting yet but will be at Presbyterian Church Sunday night and then guess we will keep it up until Xmas anyhow. After that the weather is generally so bad that we close it until in spring of the year. Yes I do hope that the Presbyterian meeting will be more successful than ours was.

Has Uncle George got his divorce? You say he is back to the city again a young man. Guess he will call on you Sunday if he knows you are in the city. Suppose you have seen Rosa by this time. You can tell her that when I come to the city she must come to see me. I don't know when Lucy is coming up, haven't seen Mrs. Moore this week so haven't heard anything from Lucy. I guess though if she does come up about the time I want to go to the city I can leave her for a few days as I guess she will stay a good while when she comes. She seems to like it so well here.

I haven't seen Miss Lillie to say anything to her I don't think since the last time I was up at your house. There is hardly a day passes now but that somebody says something to me about getting married. Everybody seems to think I am going to get married before Xmas and I can't make them believe I am not. Guess if people keep on telling me I am going to get married I will get to believing it myself. Mr. Vansickler went to Leesburg again last Wednesday, took Mr. Walden over.

Well guess I will close for this time and you must write and tell me about how you like your new home and tell me all the news. From your loving old friend

John

Aldie Va
Nov. 14th 1899

My Dearest Lee

I have just come from church and it is after nine o'clock so guess I won't have time to write a very long letter. Mr. Wilson preached last night and tonight. Had small congregations both nights. I like Mr. Wilson right well but don't think he is a very good preacher. Hugh asked me last night how I could stand it to go to church by myself. Told him I didn't like it very much but couldn't help it. Mr. Vansickler has gone with Miss Snapp two nights. She is the new school teacher you know. Guess you have had a letter from Miss Maude as she sent down for your address. Said you didn't give her your address or she couldn't understand it or something of the kind and didn't want to make a mistake.

The idea of you thinking that I was offended at you, why you dear, sweet, child I don't believe I could get offended at anything you do for I am sure you won't do anything for me to be offended at. I suppose you have found a boarding house by now. Hope you will get a place where it will be pleasant for you, Next time you go to Mrs. Imlay's give them my kindest regards and give my love to Ethel. If you room with Mrs. Russell guess she won't let you get lonesome. And then I reckon Uncle George will call on you right often besides all the other young men you know in the city.

But I am here and feel awfully lonely. Seems like an age since I saw you and guess I will have to come down before long. I have been thinking that maybe I could come down about the first of December just for a day or two you know. I won't put it off until Christmas for the weather might be so I couldn't come then and besides you know you are to come up here Xmas.

Bob Ogden was down Sunday. Didn't hear him mention Miss Maggie's name. Saw Miss Jane a while Sunday night and she said she had a letter from Miss Maggie and she said she expected she would spend the winter in Washington. Guess she will let you know if she does go to city. So you think it don't make any difference if Bob has gone back on Miss Maggie. There are others you say. Guess that's what you would say if we was to have a falling out. Your friend Miss Verge must have quite a nice time just going about all the time. I wonder if there isn't some attraction in Washington for her. I suppose you went to your church Sunday. I went to the Episcopal church in the morning, was no preaching in any of the other churches. We had Sunday School in morning and then at night there was prayer meeting at the Presbyterian church.

Now I hope you won't think I have put off answering your letter any longer than I could help for it surely is a great pleasure to write to you and I will write just as often as I can and you must do the same. I expect you will find some mistakes in this letter for I have caught myself making mistakes several times but I know you will excuse all mistakes and also bad writing. And write real soon to your loving friend

John

TO: *Miss E. L. Goode, 39 S. Street N.W., Washington, D.C.*

Aldie Va
Nov 17th 1899

My Dearest Lee

Just back from church again and just nine o'clock so will spend a short while writing. I received your nice letter this evening and was very glad to know that you had time to write so soon. I didn't expect to write until Sunday but got back from church early and thought that maybe I wouldn't have time to write Sunday for there is preaching in the morning, evening and at night. The meeting will close Sunday night. Mr. Wilson will leave tomorrow and Mr. Campbell will preach Sunday morning and night as it is his regular day for preaching here. It has been a very poor meeting, very small congregations and very little interest taken. Most everybody here don't like Mr. Wilson's preaching, but I like him tolerable well. I went to hear him every night.

I'm having a good deal of trouble writing this letter for this is a miserable pen. If you can't read it just keep it until I come down and I will read it for you. I don't hardly expect I can come Thanksgiving but will come if I can. If I can't come then I will come about the second Sunday in December. I guess it is right hard for you to get up so early to go to work, but then you will soon get used to it and then you won't mind if I make you get up early to your breakfast. And you think I sleep until seven o'clock. Why, that is late in the morning now.

Mr. Vansickler went to church with Miss Snapp again tonight. He likes to go with all the girls. He was over to Leesburg Wednesday night. He generally goes every Sunday and then again one night during the week

I never see Miss Lillie now to have any talk with her and she hasn't asked for your address. Will tell Miss Jane what you said the first time I see her. It surely does seem strange for you to dream about Mr. Vansickler so often. You must think about him a great deal. I reckon you never dream about me. Mr. Goode has the rooms finished, all but the painting is not done yet. And Tom is doing that now, will get through some time next week. I am still lonely without you but am not complaining for as you say I am at home with all my people while you are so far away amongst strangers, but then you need to being away from home so much I guess you don't mind it so much. But I know it is hard for you to get up so early and go to work and not get home until night but you won't have to do that very much longer I hope. Miss Jane told me last Sunday that she didn't think she would get married next spring, guessed she would put it off a while longer.

Well I expect I had better say goodbye and close for this old pen is just something awful. Take good care of yourself and be a nice little girl and don't fail to write to me real soon.

From your true loving friend

John

TO: Miss E L. Goode, 39 S. St. N.W., Washington, D.C.

Aldie Va
Nov 27th 1899

My Dearest Lee

I received both of your nice letters, one Saturday evening and the other one this evening and you can imagine how glad I was to hear from you again. I had commenced to think that there was something the matter, that maybe you were sick and not able to write. Well you said you hadn't been feeling very well, guess you have been working too hard. I am longing for the time to come when I see your sweet face and look into your pretty eyes and hear your kind voice again. Am very sorry I can't come next Thursday but it will not be convenient for me to leave the shop this week for Frank is going to do some work up to Dr. Thomas' so he will be away from the shop at that time and we can't both leave the shop at the same time. I want to come next Saturday week if it is so I can leave at that time.

I suppose Uncle George has been to see you before this. Guess he didn't like you not going to Baltimore with him but he ought not expect you to go with him even if he has got divorce from his wife. I am real glad you didn't go with him. I wish I could come down while George is in the city for I would like real well to see him. You must give him my kindest regards.

I can't bring you any chestnuts when I do come for I haven't any and there are none about here to be had but I will bring another big apple. I have the one you brought me from Md yet. It is still hard, guess it will keep all winter. Nearly all the children at the Goodes have been sick with sore throats but think they are all better now except Nellie. She is still right sick. I was at the drug store awhile last night and Miss Maude and Miss Jane came in for some medicine for the children and said Nellie was right sick. She was little better this morning. Miss Jane is staying there now.

Now I want to tell you something awful that happened in Middleburg last Saturday night. There was a big crowd about town and some were drinking and they got very noisy. So the police arrested one of them that was making the most noise and using bad language but he promised to behave himself and they let him go. But he went home and told his brother about it and so he came up to where the policeman was standing on Mr. Adam's porch and without saying anything he had a large knife or a razor in his hand and cut the policeman awful bad so bad that the doctor don't think he will live, and the worst of it is the man got away and they haven't caught him yet. But I guess they will get him. I expect that you know the man that was the policeman. His home is at North Fork but he has been living in Middleburg for two or three years. He is Mr. Sam Seaton's son. I think his name is Milton, I never knew him very well but he was very well thought of by everybody at Middleburg. It will be hard on his people if he should die for his mother just died a short while ago. You remember we met Mrs. Carter when you were going home, had been up to see her. He was making preparations to leave Middleburg the first of the year and go back to North Fork.

Mr. Stanton's father died last week and he has gone home to attend the funeral. He lived over in the valley near Woodstock. I think he died suddenly. Mr. John Hensley hasn't gone to the city yet. Haven't heard him say anything about going but I don't see him very often. I don't go to drug store only once in a while on Sundays and he is hardly ever home then. He has two sweethearts to go to see and it keeps him quite busy. Hugh and Miss Lillie are just the same. Her brother and a young lady from Haymarket were up to see her yesterday. I haven't heard anything about Lucy coming up lately. The last time Miss Moore said anything about her she didn't know when she was coming if at all but if she does come when I get ready to come to the city I will come just the same, that is if you don't find another fellow before I can come.

Yes Miss Snapp is quite young. Mr. Vansickler has gone to Baltimore. Went to Leesburg yesterday evening and stayed all night. Took the early train this morning. Frank Jackson went to Leesburg with him and brought the buggy and horse back and is going over again Wednesday after him. They go every Sunday and Mr. Vansickler generally goes one evening during the week. Jackson has changed his mind a good deal about going so often. Guess he would have gone oftener before if he had had as convenient way to go as he has now. I guess Miss Fannie don't know Mr. Vansickler goes with any other girls for they say she is awfully jealous. She isn't like you for you allow me to go with Miss Jane and Miss Maude but I don't see them very often. Now you must write as soon as you can for it is a very great pleasure to receive your nice letters. With much love I am as ever your own

John

Aldie Va
Dec 14th 1899

My Dearest Lee

Your long expected letter has arrived at last. I was beginning to think you had forgotten me altogether and wasn't going to write at all. I am real nervous tonight so I can hardly write at all. I don't know what is the cause of it but guess you will say it comes from using too much tobacco. I don't think that is the cause though for I haven't smoked any for two weeks.

I saw Miss Maude and Miss Jane Sunday night. I was up at Mr. Goode's a while. Hadn't been there for quite a good while, I don't think since you were there. I had a very pleasant time but not like when you were here and it does seem like a long time since I saw you. But have about made up my mind to come down Saturday if I can get off but I guess you don't look for me down now before Christmas. I had rather come before if I can as I always like to be home at Xmas.

Frank is still at Dr. Thomas's but says maybe he will get through Friday so if he does I guess I will come Saturday, but don't expect I will see you until Sunday morning but will see when I get to Alexandria. If convenient I may come over Saturday just for a little while. If I do will be there between six and seven o'clock. You must not expect me though until you see me for something may happen so I can't get off. Miss Maude said she didn't have time to write to you when the children were all sick. I think Annie is sick now. She came home from school yesterday feeling badly and today Mr. Goode said she was right poorly. I don't know when Lucy is coming up. I haven't seen any of the Moores this week but think it likely she will come Saturday or the first of next week. It would be right bad for me to go to city just when she comes but guess she will stay a good while when she comes. I have heard of Gibb Hutchison but don't know him. I thought Miss Maggie Thompson was in the city at least I heard she was and that Bob was very anxious to go down this week so he must still think something of her.

Well I expect I will close for this time and if I possibly can I will come Saturday and I think now I can get off all right. We are not so very busy and if Frank can come to the shop why I can leave all right.

Guess I can't stay but a few days though. If I don't come don't be disappointed and write me a nice letter real soon. With much love I am as ever your true

John

Aldie Va
Dec 17th 1899

My Dear Lee

I expect you were a little disappointed again about me not coming Saturday but Frank didn't get through at Dr. Thomas' and there was a good deal of work at the shop and I didn't think it right for me to leave. But Frank only has one or two more days work and then he will be done and will be at the shop and I can leave and am surely coming next Thursday or Friday if the trains run and maybe I will stay until after Xmas. We won't have a Christmas tree so there will be nothing to keep me here except that I always would rather spend Xmas at home but have never had an opportunity to spend Xmas in such pleasant company as I will this time. That is if you don't get tired seeing me before that time. You will please write me as soon as you get this and let me know if you will be home Friday night or if you will be at work. If at home I will come over.

Annie Goode has the scarlet fever and all the people that have children at home are most scared to death that they will catch it. The school has closed until after Xmas.

There is to be a wedding at the Methodist church here next Wednesday. I am to be an usher. Guess I will see the little dressmaker for I think she is to attend the bride. Mr. Stanton is to marry them. Well I won't write any more this time but will tell you all the news I know when I see you. Now don't forget to write right away so I will get the letter Wednesday as I may want to start on Thursday. Lovingly

John

Aldie Va
Dec 19th 1899

Dearest Lee

Your letter received this evening and very glad to hear from you so soon though I expected a letter yesterday. I am awfully sorry to disappoint you so often but then we all have our disappointments in this life. But I don't think I will disappoint you this time for I expect to go to Alexandria Thursday but won't get to Washington until Friday. By the time I get there it will be about 4 o'clock and then I don't like to go right straight away again. They might not like it for the last time I was there they told me I spent all my time in Washington so will stay in Alexandria Thursday night and go to Washington Friday evening some time so I will be there early, say about half past six or not later than seven.

Tomorrow is the day for the wedding here and looks now as if it would be a nice day after raining all day long today. I'll do as you say and not tell them when I am coming home but don't think I can stay very long, maybe until about Wednesday if you will let me stay that long. Harry Palmer and John Hensley wanted me to wait until New Years and go down with them but told them I couldn't wait. I had no idea I would put it off as long as I have. Now you may expect me Friday night and if I don't come you may know that something serious has happened. Goodbye from,

John

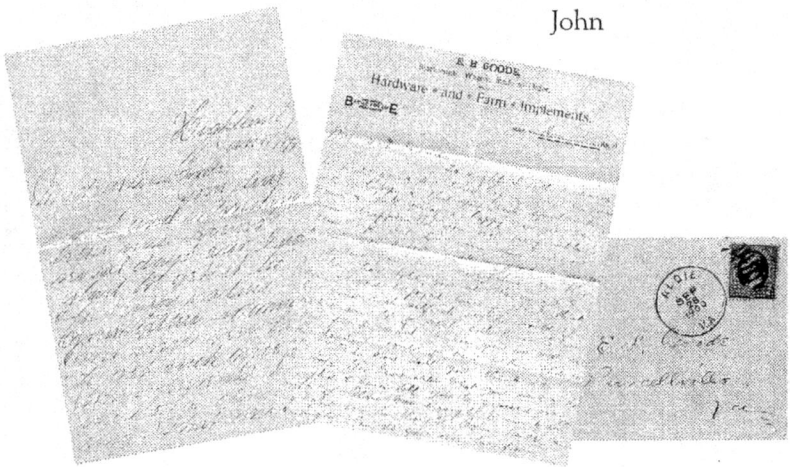

1900

Aldie Va.
Jan 14th, 1900

My Dear Lee,

This has been a lovely day except that it is quite muddy in the roads but it has been a very dull Sunday for me, no place to go all the afternoon. I started up to see Miss Maude and when I got to the drug store she and the children were just coming out of the front gate so I stopped at drug store. They just went for a walk but stayed a good while so I thought I would come home and write to you and maybe I will go up there tonight. Miss Maude hasn't been to Sunday Schcol since Annie was sick and none of the children hadn't been coming until today. Mary and Willie came.

Charlie Carter died last Thursday morning about half past eight o'clock and was buried Friday evening at Middleburg. It was a very stormy evening. Snowed until we were about half way to Middleburg and then cleared off very nice. Mr. and Mrs. Carter took it very hard. Mr. Stanton conducted the funeral services at the church. He told me that Miss Annie Kerrick died a few days before with typhoid fever. I am not sure though if he said Annie but think he did. Said she had been delicate most all her life.

I suppose you will be here to go to quarterly meeting next Sunday and Monday. You remember you told me you would come up and go with me so if you don't come I will be badly disappointed you know. Mr. Vansickler reminded me today of old times when you were here. He went to church with Miss Fannie this morning and then this afternoon they went out driving and suppose he will go to see her again tonight unless she tells him not to come. Excuse me I am not to say any more about that but I wrote that before I thought about it but won't mention it any more. I don't know whether you can read this or not. I can't hardly read it myself but if you can't just keep it until I see you again and I will read it to you. Seems like the lines are too close together on this paper and this old pen is just awful.

Yes Gene Downs is still at Mr. Goode's and Frank Jackson isn't doing anything. Don't know what he intends to do but there is some talk of him building a shop here. I think though it is just talk. I will try and get Miss Jone's address for you if you want to send Uncle George around to call on her. It would be a very pleasant surprise to me to hear that they had run off and gotten married but don't think you would like as well as you pretend for he wouldn't give you any more rings then. Did I tell you in my last letter about Miss Carrie Pearson and Mr. Mitchell going to city and getting married? I saw him Friday when I went to the funeral and asked him why he didn't tell Mr. Prisson they were going to be married. He said he told him last summer and didn't think it worth while to tell him again. Mr. Prisson was very much opposed to it and won't let them come to his house but guess he will get over it after awhiles.

I expect I had better stop for this time because maybe you can't read it anyway. Will try and have a better pen next time. Write soon to your loving friend

John

P.S. I forgot to put the account of Hugh's wedding in last letter so will put it in this and send pictures soon. John

---

TO: *Miss E. L. Goode, 39 S. St., N.W., Washington, D.C*

Aldie, Va.
Jan 28th, 1900

My Dearest Lee,

It has been right cold for a few days, but guess you haven't felt it much in the city as it never seems as cold as it does in the country. This is a very dull day here, no preaching at all. I went to Sunday School this morning. Miss Maude was there for the first time this year. She asked me if I had heard from you lately, and she had written to you a few days ago but hadn't had time to hear from you. Said she had asked you to come up here instead of going to Maryland, that you had said you were thinking of going to Maryland. She said she hoped you would come up here, it was so lonely. I told her I hoped you would come too. I asked her if she knew when Miss Jane was

Children of George and Margaret Bodmer all born in Virginia:

1. Mary   b. 1857; not married
2. Catherine   b. Jan 13, 1859; d. Sept 9, 1922; not married
3. George   b. Aug 1864; not married
4. John W.   b. 8/30/1868; d. Feb 2, 1944; m. Ella Lee Goode
5. Charles   b. April 16, 1871; d. July 20, 1894; not married
6. James F.   b. Aug 29, 1873; d. 1947; m. Alice W. Bodmer
7. Thomas   b. Jan 25, 1876; m. 1.Effie Mae Hutchison;
                         2. Henrietta Moran
8. Lewis H.   b. May 22, 1878; d. Sept 29, 1905
9. Robert L.   b. April 25, 1881; not married

Information from gravemarkers at Middleburg Memorial Cemetery and the 1900 Federal Census for Loudoun County.

---

coming home as the lady she was nursing died last Friday and was buried today at Ebenezer. She said that she thought she would stay in the city for awhile at her sister's, Mrs. Hough at Brookland. I wouldn't be surprised if she came home any day for she don't like to stay away from Aldie for very long at a time.

Have you found out where Rosa is working? Sorry to hear you had such a bad cold. Hope it is better by this time. I haven't had a real bad cold this winter. Was glad to hear that you have been going around some. Next time you see Edie give my love to her and remember me to Mr. Tew and Frank. Hugh and Mrs. Bruin, I mean Mrs. Hugh Bruin, have gone to Haymarket today and I think she is going to stay home a week. I think I will have to go to Mrs. Goode's again tonight. It is so lonesome today, no place to go. Guess the children will entertain me for a while if I go. Randolph talks real plain now. You ought to hear him say Maudie. Says it as plain as anybody.

I think you had better mind your Ma and go home for awhile if you haven't much work. But you must come by way of Aldie. It is nearer anyway to come here first and then go to Purcellville and it would be such a nice drive to Leesburg and back, especially coming home. But I expect though you would rather go to Maryland. I am going to try and send you that picture tomorrow so you will get it same time you get this. If I don't I will surely send it one day this week. Have just been putting off sending it from time to time.

I guess Lucy is like most all other girls, likes the city fellows best. Frank Jackson is working for Mr. Goode again just for a few days. Mr. Goode has a very sore hand, burnt it on hot iron. I think Jackson is anxious to hire to Mr. Goode again and I expect he will hire him. John Hensley is having more bad luck. He has stopped going with Miss Anderson, don't know what the trouble is. He still goes with Miss Snapp but the old doctor says she don't care a snap for him. Don't know what he will do when school closes and she goes home. He won't have any girl at all but guess he can find one.

I don't know when I can come to city but would like to come soon. Will wait though until you find out if you are going to Maryland or coming up here or going home. And if you stay in the city I will try and get down some time next month if the weather don't get too bad. It looks now as if it might snow soon but hope it won't.

I will have to say goodbye for I have written out. Write soon to your loving friend (excuse my handwriting)

John

TO: Miss E. L. Goode, 39 S. St., N.W., Washington, D.C.

Aldie Va
Feb 4th, 1900

My Dearest Lee,

I received your nice sweet letter Friday evening and will try and answer it today as usual. I have just come from church and it is raining real hard so think this a good time to write. I didn't take an umbrella so had to come home in the rain. I had my overcoat though so didn't get wet. Mrs. Stanton came down with Mr. Stanton. Guess they will get wet going home. Miss Jane is home again. Came last Wednesday or Thursday. She is staying with Mrs. Moore next door today and yesterday. Saw her pass the shop late yesterday evening and asked me to come to see her, but I couldn't go. Saw her at church again this evening and asked me again to come to see her tonight. I may go over there a while tonight if it stops raining. I don't go in the rain to see many people but I guess you know I don't stop for rain sometimes. Mr. Moore has gone to see his mother. She is very sick, not expected to live long. Haven't seen Maude since last Sunday night. Was not at Sunday school this morning. She had company, two of her brothers and her mother came down yesterday evening. I think Mrs. Ellison is going to stay for a while. I was up there last Sunday night, had a real pleasant time. Mrs. Goode wanted to know when I was going to meet the train. I told her as soon as the train comes I was going to meet it. They all expect you to come up soon.

They are to have another new school teacher here. Miss Yates is going to give up the school. I think tomorrow is her last day to teach. The new teacher is a Miss Rogers from Hamilton, maybe you know her. Miss Yates has gotten homesick and won't stay any longer.

Mrs. Hugh Bruin didn't stay home very long. Came back Friday morning. I suppose you will know by the time you write again when you are coming up. You say I expect you to come up here when the weather is too bad for me to go to the city. Well you know I would never think the weather too bad for me to come but don't like to ask one of the boys to take me to Leesburg and then after I would get to city might come another blizzard so I couldn't get home. But you could come up here and if it did come a blizzard you could stay until it was over. There would be somebody to meet you if you come and I don't think it would be Mr. Hensley either unless you don't let anybody else know when you come.

Am real glad Rosa has a nice place to work but as you say it she has to be there most all the time. Don't guess it will suit her very well. Tell Miss Katie that when she comes up I will meet her at Leesburg, that I know you wouldn't object. But maybe she meant she wouldn't ride with me and if she won't why we can get Mr. Hensley to go over after her. I know he would go. He has gone somewhere this evening, went down the pike and nobody can guess where he has gone. Guess he has a new girl that we don't know about. You can tell Miss Katie about him and tell her I know he would like her. I wonder what has become of Uncle George. Don't you think you had better go and look him up? He might have another girl and that is the reason he hasn't been to see you any oftener than he has. I wish he could have met Miss Jane while he was in city. I guess the reason she didn't come to see you was because she didn't have your address but will ask her when I see her.

Frank's baby is right sick. Has been for three or four days and is no better today. I suppose you haven't received the picture yet and I felt awfully ashamed for not sending it. Just put it off from day to day but will surely send it this week. Mr. Jackson has stopped working for Mr. Goode again, only worked a few days while his hand was sore. Don't think Mr. Goode wants him before the first of March as I heard him say he would hire him then if he didn't get another place. I don't think he wants to leave Aldie this year. Mr. Vansickler went to Leesburg this morning. Will have a rainy time coming home tonight if it don't stop raining. Well they have just called me to supper so guess I will close as I don't know anything else to write. When you get ready to come up let me know a day or two before you come and I will be at Leesburg when the train comes. Write real soon to your loving friend

John B.

TO: *Miss E. L. Goode, 39 S St., N. W., Washington, D.C.*

Aldie Va
Feb. 11th 1900
Sunday Night

My Dearest Lee

I have just come home from Mr. Goode's and it is a few minutes past nine o'clock so don't think will have time to write a very long letter. You see I don't stay up as late as I used to last summer and fall. I was at the drug store and Gene Downs came in and told me Miss Jane was up to the home so thought I would go up and see her as I hadn't seen her since she came home only just to speak to her. I asked her why she didn't go to see you while she was in the city and she said she didn't have your address. Thought you ought to have gone to see her. Seems strange so many people you know go to city and never go to see you, but there is one that never fails to find you whenever in the city. This has been such a lovely day and I wished several times I was down there instead of here.

They are still looking for you to come up at Mr. Goode's. Mrs. Goode said you wrote as though you would come this week, but I told her I didn't think you expected to come any time soon from what you wrote me. She seemed to be very much disappointed when I told her you didn't think you could come. They all seem right downhearted about Annie. She is sick again and they think she might be getting the typhoid fever but I surely hope she is not. She surely does have a lot of sickness. Mrs. Goode has a sore thumb that is giving her a great deal of trouble. Mrs. Ellison is there, came last Sunday. I came home as Miss Jane did. She said she guessed you wouldn't object to me going home with her. I asked Maude what you told me and she told me to tell you yes she would but wouldn't tell me what it was you wanted her to do. Seemed to think at first that I knew but I told her I didn't.

Frank's baby is still quite sick. Has the whooping cough now and today it had a spasm. Frank was away and Alice was nearly frightened to death. I was up there a while tonight before I went to Mr. Goode's and it seemed to be a little better. There is a good deal of whooping cough around here amongst the children. Miss Maude says she never had it and is afraid she will have it now. I told her I expect she will have it with the rest of the children.

We had a wedding here last Thursday, at least the couple that were married live here. Mr. Fry and Miss Ida Jackson. They went to Leesburg and were married there. Didn't tell anybody but their own people and not all of them. Never told Mr. Bill Jackson at all. We all expected it though and gave them a serenade that night. Frank Jackson will have to get married now. When Mr. Fry takes Miss Ida away won't be anybody but old Mrs. Jackson and she is real old. Went to Leesburg today so guess he is thinking about getting married. Think he is going back to work for Mr. Goode first of March but am not sure.

Tell Rosa will try and let her know when I come to city for I want to see her real badly. I don't know if I can come before Conference or not but will if I can. I believe the Conference is to meet the fourth of April at Mt. Vernon Church but I guess you knew that. Harry Palmer came home yesterday, said he went to Mt. Vernon every Sunday morning but never saw you, so guess you haven't been going to church very much this year. If you decide to come up any time let me know so I can meet you at Leesburg. Hope you can come for I think it would do you good to get out of the city for a while and then it seems so long since I saw you and if you came up here and stayed a while I can wait until conference before I go to city. But if you don't come I may have to come before that time.

Well expect I had better stop for this time. Will write more next time. Hope you will get this Monday. Seems so strange you hardly ever get my letters until the next day. I received your letter Friday as usual. Trusting to hear from you real soon I am as ever your loving

John B.

Aldie, Va
Feb 15th, 1900

My Dearest Lee,

I received your nice letter yesterday evening and was a little surprised to hear from you so soon. Was very glad to hear from you but very sorry you don't think you can come up at all this winter and Mrs. Goode is very badly disappointed about it. She has such a sore thumb. I think she has a bone felon on her thumb so she can't do any sewing and she expected you to come up and help her with her sewing. I don't know why they have been expecting you unless you wrote them different from what you wrote me and I told them Sunday night that you said you didn't think you could come. But yesterday Mrs. Ellison was down here and said they were still expecting you to come up sometime and asked Mother if she had heard me say when you were coming. Annie is getting better but is still right sick. The doctor don't think she will have the fever but he was right uneasy about her for a few days. She surely does have lots of sickness. Frank's baby is better too and they think it will be all right now in a few days. Still has the whooping cough but not very bad.

Would like very much to come to see you next Saturday and Sunday but it won't be as I can come and besides it is Mr. Stanton's day to preach here and I don't like to be away preaching days. He only has 4 more times to preach here before conference and he don't expect to come back another year so I want to hear him every time. Wish you could come and hear him before he goes away. It might be so I can come Sunday week, if it is so I can I will let you know. I don't believe you care to come up here any more.

Don't think I would go to Leesburg to get married. Guess I would go to Washington like most everybody else from about here does. Guess Mr. Fry didn't have time to go any further than Leesburg for he had to go to work next day after he was married. The new school teacher is getting along real well and think all the scholars like her. She is real small, not any larger than Miss Maude. Don't think John Hensley has called on her yet. Don't know of any young men have called on her but guess John will before long if he has time. He has a girl out of town somewhere but I don't know who she is. He goes to see her every Sunday and I think he went last night. Bally went to see his girl last night. He went along just as I was going to the store. It will be very nice for Willie Goode to be in the city and come to see you every Sunday but guess he will soon have a girl to go to see. Did you know Mr. Lewis? He was taken suddenly sick last Sunday and is still very sick, has two doctors tending him, Dr. Thomas and Dr. Lusk. He is right old and not likely to get well.

Do you ever hear from Mr. and Mrs. Seaton? I mean Blanche. How are they getting along and all the rest of your people. How is your Grandmother? Give my love to them all next time you write to them. Harry Palmer is home now but says he is going to have to go to city soon. Well I can't think of anything else to write so will have to close. Write soon to your loving friend

John

TO: *Miss E. G. Goode, 39 S St., N.W., Washington, D.C.*

Aldie Va
Feb 21st 1900

My Dearest Lee

I received your very nice and much appreciated letter Monday evening and would have answered it last night but went to the store and played dominoes until most ten o'clock and then it was too late to write after I got home. This surely has been a very disagreeable day and it is still raining hard, looks as if it would rain all night. Guess the snow will soon go off if it rains all night and stays warm. I expect we had more snow up here than there was in the city, it was about twenty inches deep and drifted right badly but nothing like it was last winter. Some of the roads have some deep drifts in them so that people can only travel horseback. The mail carrier to Leesburg has been going horseback, only one day went in a sleigh. It takes him until most night to get back here. John Hensley started to Leesburg in his buggy today. Took him until twelve o'clock to get to Oatlands and then he got into a snowdrift and broke the shafts of his buggy. Guess it will be bad traveling for some time so don't look for me this week. I am very sorry but I guess I can't come for two or three weeks but will come as soon as I can. It seems like an age since I saw you but when the roads are good I will try and see you oftener than I have this winter. Hope you are over your case of homesickness by now and wish you had come up before the snow came and you could have stayed until it was all gone.

I saw Mrs. Goode yesterday evening, came down to the blacksmith shop to go home with Mr. Goode. Said Miss Jane was up Sunday night and had music and singing. I stayed home it was so cold and snow was so deep. Didn't have Sunday School or preaching either. Sunday Mr. Campbell or Mr. Stanton neither one came. Annie Goode is much better than she was but is still right sick and Frank's baby has gotten well except coughs some yet. I didn't go sleigh riding at all, didn't care to go but would have if you had been here if you would have gone with me. Lew went yesterday evening. Took Miss Anderson, Mr. Gulick's governess. Upset the sleigh in a snow drift and threw her out but didn't get hurt.

Well you got more valentines than I did for I never got a single one. I think Miss Jane got one or two. Hugh Bruin fell down on the stone porch yesterday and struck the side of his head on door sill. Hurt him right bad but he was at the store part of the day today. I wonder where the Davis boys heard you were going to get married. Tell your Ma that you will let her know when you are going to be married and that people hardly ever go to Aldie to get married. Most all go to Washington or Leesburg or Hamilton. No Mr. Ball and Mr. Vansickler have not gone back to Uncle Ed's. Are boarding at Mr. Jerega's.

I don't think Bob Ogden ever goes down to see Miss Thompson as I saw him two or three weeks ago and he said he hadn't seen her but once since camp meeting. I don't think they are to be married very soon if at all but then we can't always tell. Mrs. Fry is still at home and I heard somebody say she was going to stay here in Aldie all the year. Frank Jackson is going back to work for Mr. Goode the first of March. I surely do hope it will be so I can come to see you before very long but if I don't come it won't be because I don't want to. If there was railroad here I could come real often. Now be a good little girl and write to me real soon.

From you loving friend

John

TO: *Miss E. L. Goode, 39 S St., N.W., Washington, D.C.*

Aldie Va
March 4, 1900

My Dear Lee

I don't know whether I ought to write to you today or not after the way you treated me last week. I looked for a letter the first of the week and it never came until Friday. I was awfully disappointed until your letter came and after I read it I was worse disappointed than ever, just a few lines and never said why you hadn't written sooner. Seemed to me some one must have come in while you were writing and you stopped before you finished what you had intended to write. I have been in very poor spirits ever since but feel better now since going to church and hearing Mr. Stanton preach. His sermon just suited me. He said that we all have our trials and disappointments in this world but that if we are only faithful we shall overcome all the trials and temptations of this world and obtain a crown of life after death. He will only preach here twice more, the third Sunday and first Sunday in April. He don't expect to come back after Conference. I don't know if I will come to the city before that time or not and it depends on you if I come then. The way you talked in your letter you didn't seem to care whether I came at all or not and if you don't care to see me I don't think I will ever go to Washington again, certainly not soon. I don't suppose Miss Maude told you any harm about Miss Jane and myself. I was at Mrs. Goode's again last Sunday night and Miss Jane was there. Stayed until about half past nine and then went home with Miss Jane, that is, I went as far as her gate.

You surely are improving in your writing. The address on envelope of last letter was ever so much better than you used to write. This has been a lovely day and if I was sure you were the same to me that you used to be I would have liked to have been in the city and if next

Sunday is a nice day I may come anyway. Go down on early train and back at night. Mr. Goode asked me yesterday when I was going to city again and this morning Miss Maude asked me the same question. I don't know why they want to know. I think they are all well at Mr. Goode's now. Annie don't go out yet but she seemed to be right well last Sunday night. Mrs. J. Moore was right sick for a few days last week but is better again. There was a man fall dead in Middleburg today, was a shoemaker named Kelley. He was sitting in a chair talking and just dropped dead without a moment's warning. Well I don't know anything else to write so will close and trust you will find time and opportunity to answer this sooner than you did last week.

From your loving friend

John

TO: *Miss E. L. Goode, 39 S St., N.W., Washington, D.C.*

Aldie Va
March 8th 1900

My Dearest Lee

I received your nice sweet letter yesterday evening and how glad I was to hear from you again so soon. I guess you thought I was in a bad humor when I wrote the last letter but I wasn't, only a little downhearted because you waited so long before you wrote last week and then wrote such a short letter that I thought you had forsaken me. I am ashamed of myself for thinking that but it kept coming in my mind and I couldn't get rid of the thought. I see how foolish it was in me to think that way. But yesterday when I read your nice letter I felt greatly relieved and if you will forgive me for the way I wrote to you I will try and never do so again. I don't know exactly what I did write but hope I didn't say anything mean. But if I did I am awfully sorry for I wouldn't say or do anything to hurt your feelings for anything in this world. I don't remember waiting very long before writing to you. You say it was nearly two weeks but it surely couldn't have been near that long, but did wait a day or two longer than I would have if it hadn't been for the snow. I didn't think the mail would go on Monday so didn't write on Sunday as I had intended to do but think I wrote Monday night and mailed it Tuesday morning.

I am not sure if I can come Sunday or not but will surely come if I can get anybody to go to Leesburg with me. I wouldn't like to go alone so soon in the morning and then it would be late at night to come home from Leesburg. I think the train gets to Leesburg about eight o'clock Sundays. I know it is later than on week days. If I come I will be obliged to come back same day. Guess I will get there before you are up if you sleep late on Sundays.

You must not think that I go with Miss Jane very often. I haven't been to her house since Xmas, only saw her at Mr. Goode's two or three times. I didn't see her at all last Sunday. She didn't come to Sunday School. Hugh and Mrs. Bruin are going to Baltimore about the first week in April to buy their millinery goods. He is going to stop clerking for Mr. Wrenn first of April. I don't know what he is going to do after that but think he would start a store of his own if he had a place. I guess they will call to see you while in Washington for I think they are going to stop a few days in Washington before they go to Baltimore.

I will let Mrs. Goode know if I come down Sunday. You mustn't expect me until you see me for something might happen so that I can't come. If I don't come Sunday I don't expect I will come until Conference and that won't be long now, just four weeks. Well I can't think of anything else to write so guess I had better close. Trusting to see you soon or to hear from you I am as ever your loving friend

John

TO: Miss E. L. Goode, 39 S St., N.W., Washington, D.C.

Aldie Va
Sunday Eve,
March 18th 1900

My Dear Lee

What has become of you anyhow? Have you forgotten me entirely? It seems like you have for I haven't heard from you since week

The Bodmer shop and family home in Aldie, VA. The buildings still stand along the Little River.

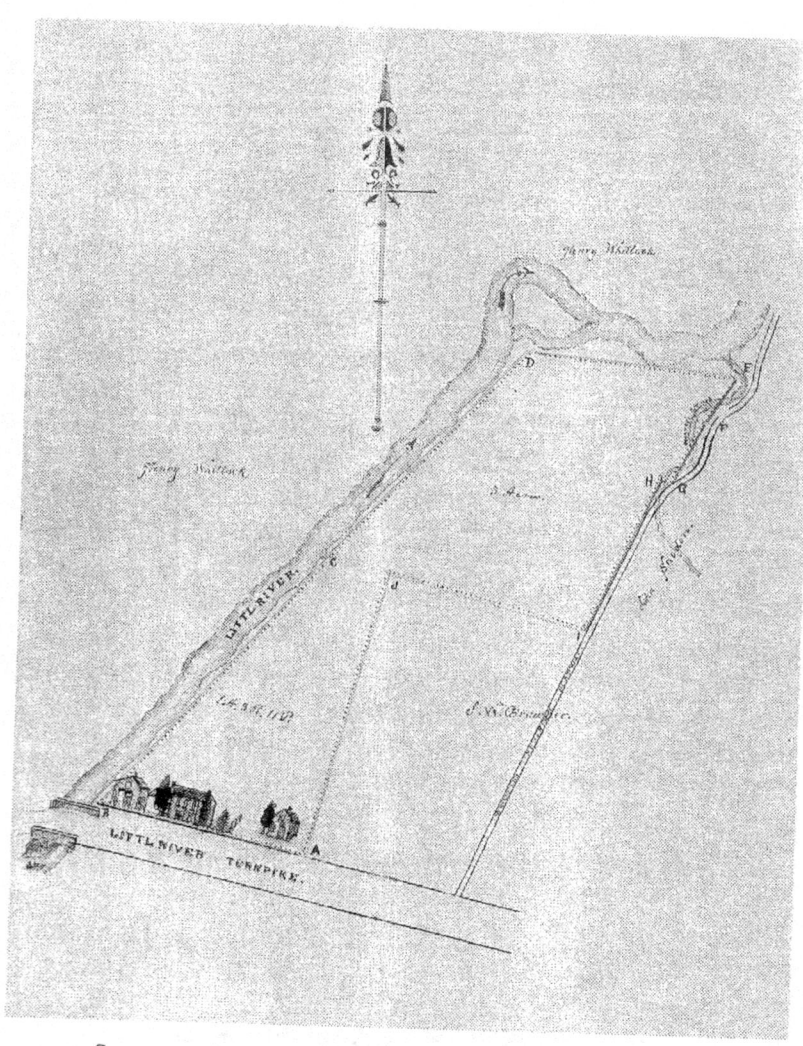

Survey to the Bodmer property along Little River in Aldie

B.C, &c.   Thence with the Water line on the eastern part of
Little River & Southern canal of _____ County to (C.)
a set Stone 74 links ___ on the _____ of _____ _____
corner with Henry Whitlock.

C.D.   Thence with Henry Whitlock, S 36¼ W 110½ chains to (D)
a set Stone, corner with the same.

D.E.   Thence with Henry Whitlock, S 60 W 151½ chains to (E)
a set Stone, corner with the same.

E.F.   Thence with Henry Whitlock, N 65¼ W 20 chains to (F)
a set Stone, corner with the same.

F.G.   Thence with Henry Whitlock, S 25¾ W 36 chains to (G)
a set Stone, corner with James W. Browne in the line of
Whitlock's second tract survey.

G.H.   Thence with James W. Browne N 75¼ W 438 chains
to (H) a set Stone, corner with the same.

H.A.   Thence with James W. Browne, S 12¼ W 114½ chains
to (A) the beginning.   (B, C &c.)

_____

Containing 4 acres 3 Roods 11 Poles.

James S. Orton S.B.C
June 25ᵗʰ 1872

The 7ᵗʰ with Capt. _____

Map & Descriptive Survey.

Bodmer George
of
Noland's B.R. commrs

———

Bodmer George
vs
Whitlock Henry

———

Lying on the north side of the Little River Turnpike
and on the eastern side of the Little River, in and adjacent
to the Village of Aldie, Township of Mercer, County of
Loudoun, State of Virginia.

A.   Beginning, at (A) the southwestern corner of the
Saddlers Shop of James W. Brawner, in the northern line
of the Little Turnpike Road.

A.B.   Thence, with the northern line of the Little River
Turnpike Road, N 7°40′ W, 4.50 chains to (B) on the
eastern bank of Little River, 30 feet north of the center
of the eastern end of the Bridge, corner with Henry
Whitlock, (lot 3 73/40).

before last. I wrote to you last Thursday a week and haven't heard from you since I wrote you that I expected to come down to see you last Sunday. But didn't get off. But I wanted to come awful bad and had made all arrangements to come. Expected to come clear up until Saturday night and then everybody told me it was going to be stormy Sunday so I concluded I had better not start. I waked up some time in the night and looked out and saw it was real cloudy so thought had better not start. I would have had a nice time coming home from Leesburg in the snow if I had gone. It seems like winter will never be over, the ground covered with snow and almost as cold as it has been any time in the winter here. It is the 18th of March. Well maybe the snow will be gone by the time I come to the city but I am not going to tell anybody when I am coming for it would be sure then to storm.

I just came from church and Mr. Stanton preached a very fine sermon. He will only preach once more, the first Sunday in April. Hugh Bruin and his wife are going to start to Baltimore the last of this week. I think they are going to spend next Sunday in Washington so guess they will call to see you. I will tell them to call anyway and if you are lost will get them to look you up. Hugh stopped clerking for Mr. Wrenn the 15th of this month. I haven't seen much of Miss Jane for some time but think she has been staying at Mr. Goode's for several days. Saw her at church this evening. She had a new ring. Said her fellow sent it to her. Saw Miss Maude at Sunday School this morning for the first time in two weeks. She wasn't at Sunday School last Sunday. Some of the boys are out sleigh riding today but the snow is most all gone off the roads. Lew was out yesterday. Went over to Mr. Gulick's and took the governess out sleighing. John Hensley has gone today. I couldn't go because I didn't have anybody to go with me and didn't care to go alone.

There was a right sudden death near here yesterday. An old man lived in a little house a little ways this side of Mt. Zion church. He was out at woodpile cutting wood and was taken sick and went to the house and died in a few minutes before the doctor could get there. He was real old, I guess about 80 years. I surely do hope you are not sick but I have been thinking maybe you are because you haven't written to me before this. Well I can't think of any news so will close trusting to hear from you real soon. I am as ever yours.

John

Aldie Va
March 20th 1900

My Dearest Lee

I received your scolding letter yesterday evening and was very glad to hear from you again if you did give me a scolding. I guess I deserved it for I ought to have written to you sooner. I thought I would write to you the day after I was to have come to the city but thought that after I didn't come you would write to me and kept looking for a letter all the week. I know you think it strange in me not to come to see you any oftener than I do but I assure you I would like to come real often but you know it is quite a good deal of trouble and expense besides. I surely did think though that I was going the Sunday I told you I was and if they all hadn't told me it was going to be a stormy day I would have come. But as it turned out I guess it is well I didn't start for it surely was a stormy day. You may know it was bad for John Hensley started to call on his lady friend and went a little ways and then came back and said it was too bad for him to travel. Mr. Vansickler went to Leesburg but said he was nearly frozen when he got home that night.

I shouldn't think you would care whether I wrote or not last week, you got so many letters from other fellows and going to theatre besides. You ought not to get a bit lonely. Hope you enjoyed yourself at theatre and I have no doubt you had a fine escort and guess you could have an escort any time you wanted to go any place if you would let Uncle George know. I am awfully sorry Miss Katie thinks me so very mean and I am sure I didn't mean to be so mean and if I didn't want to come to see you or write to you any more I surely would tell you.

Maude is still here in Aldie. I was up to call on her Sunday night. Went with Miss Jane. She was at Mrs. Moore's in the evening and after supper I walked out towards the shop and she came along going uptown and asked me if I was going up the street. Said she wanted to go to Mrs. Goode's and asked me to go along so she would have somebody to come home with her. So of course I always like to be accommodating and went along with her. We had quite a nice time, stayed until about nine o'clock. I guess Rosa thought you would be homesick and want to go home with her if she would tell you she was going home but it does seem strange she didn't tell you. Hugh just told me they are going to Washington Friday or Saturday and stay until Monday when they will go to Baltimore. So guess you will see them Sunday if they have time to come and see you.

Now you will get enough letters this week to pay up for last week and I will surely be down the last of week after next. Don't know what day yet but will let you know later. So now goodbye. Write soon. From your loving friend

John W. B.

TO: *Miss E. L. Goode, 39 S St., N.W., Washington, D.C.*

Aldie Va
March 28th 1900

My Dearest Lee

I received your nice sweet letter yesterday evening and think it the nicest letter you have written me for a long time, if you did do a little scolding. I know you have a right to scold for I guess I didn't treat you just right. I never thought much about it at the time but see now that I wouldn't have liked for you to treat me like that. But I am going to be real good now and never treat you mean again.

Don't you know Miss Jane is staying with Mrs. Moore just next door, has been there three or four days and I haven't seen her since she has been there. Mr. Moore has gone to Baltimore and she is going to stay until he comes back. Guess he will be home tomorrow evening. Oh no I don't go with Miss Jane very much, only see her at Mrs. Goode's when I go there. She just happens to be there most every time I go there and that isn't very often, about once in two or three weeks and she is only doing as you asked her to do taking care of me while you are not here. It was strange Miss Maude should address your letter wrong. Must have been something on her mind. I intended to ask her about it this morning at Sunday School but never thought of it. Hugh and Lil as he calls her are in Washington today. I guess I had intended to give them your address and tell them to go see you but forgot all about it. So don't know whether they have your address or not. They expect to stay until next Sunday or Monday.

Well I never expected you to meet those people in South West. Guess they will have a lot to tell me next time they see me for the old gentleman is a great tease. Told you I had told him all about you but I hadn't told him a thing about you. He did tell me which way to go the first night I came to see you on S St. Their name is Colison and live on Sixth St., No 823. I don't think I told you they went to church at 9th and P. They were only talking about the members of that church. They always go to some church in S.W. but I never knew where it was. Guess it's a Northern Methodist. I suppose Rosa has gotten back to city by this time. If she hasn't guess she will be back by next Christmas when I come down.

This has been a cold disagreeable day but not bad enough to keep Mr. Vansickler from going to Leesburg. Mr. Jackson went with him, didn't start until about 2 o'clock. I expect to go to Haymarket tomorrow after some buggies. Hope it will be a nice day but don't look now like it would. Looks like it will rain tonight or tomorrow. I went to the Episcopal Church this afternoon and heard a very good sermon. Next Sunday Mr. Stanton will preach his last sermon before Conference and I expect it will be the last time he will ever preach here. I will try and come to the city next Christmas if I can arrange to leave home at that time and the weather is good. Guess I had better close for this time. Trusting to hear from you real soon. I am as ever your loving friend

John

TO: Miss E. L. Goode, 39 S St., N.W., Washington, D.C.

Aldie Va
Apr 12th 1900

My Dearest Lee

Well I got home all safe but don't you know I walked from Leesburg clear home, never anyone came to meet me. Said they were not sure whether I was coming or not as they had not heard anything from me. Sent me word by stagedriver to telephone over if I came and Lew would come over for me but I thought I wouldn't put them to the trouble. Thought I would just walk along until the stage overtook me and then I would get in and ride the balance of the way. But the stage never overtaken me and I just kept on and got home before the stage got here. I didn't mind the walk very much but was right tired when I got here. I don't think I want to undertake to walk again. It rained most all the way, but I didn't get wet only my overcoat got a little wet.

I suppose you know who our new preacher is by now. I am real anxious to see him and hear him preach. I learned who he was before I left Washington that night. Asked a preacher on the car. He said he was a real good preacher and thought we would all like him. Mrs. Wrenn knows of him and has heard him preach, says he is a much better preacher than Mr. Stanton but if he is as good we will all be satisfied with him. I suppose you have noticed that Mr. Stevens is to go to Marvin Chapel corner 10th and B Sts S.W. You must go and hear him sometimes, am sure you would like him. I haven't seen Miss Jane yet, don't even know if she is home or not. I asked Gene Downs and he said he didn't know where she was. Mr. Goode wanted to know why you didn't come up with me. Mrs. Moore hasn't gone to Alexandria, had a letter from Lucy saying she had the whooping cough and is afraid if she takes Hubert her little boy you know down there he will take it. She is waiting to hear from her again to know if she really has whooping cough. She wants to go but if she has only a cold she thinks she will go Sunday. Think I will go along with her if she does go. Mr. Vansickler came back from Baltimore today. They say he is to be married in June or July.

I have missed you so much since coming home. Wish I had stayed until today. Well I will have to close for this time as it is getting late and you know I haven't been in the habit of sitting up late. Was over to Mrs. Moore's and stayed longer than I intended. Will write more next time if I know of anything to write. You must write real soon. From your true, loving friend

John

Aldie Va
Apr 22nd 1900

My Dear Lee

I was a little surprised to get your letter yesterday but I about halfway expected you would write before Sunday. There wasn't any preaching here today only at the Episcopal Church at 4 o'clock. There wasn't very many there, looked so much like rain just before preaching that didn't many go. Mr. Smith preached a real good sermon though if there wasn't many to hear him. Mr. Vansickler went to Leesburg this evening, started just before it commenced to rain. He don't mind going in bad weather like another fellow I know. I believe I have about gotten over the spring fever, at least I feel all right again. I went to Sunday School this morning, wonder if you did. Miss Maude was there and asked me to come up before Miss Snapp goes home. She will only be there one more Sunday and maybe Mr. Anderson will come next Sunday so I told her that I would come up tonight maybe. I guess John Hensley will be there as he spends most of his time there Sundays. If I go I will let you know when I come back tonight.

I hope Miss Nettie doesn't dislike me. I don't see why she should but if she does I'm sure it is no fault of mine. I was over to Mrs. Bruin's millinery shop one day last week. She asked me about you, wanted to know when you were coming. I told her I didn't know. She said she was going to write to you that night so guess you have heard from her before this. It seems awful strange of Rosa to not let you know where she is anytime. Guess she is having a good time. I haven't seen Miss Jane yet, she is at Mr. Douglass's now. They are most all sick there. Mr. Douglass and Mrs. Douglass and little girl all sick at same time but are all getting better now. Mabel Palmer has been right sick too but is better now. There has been a good deal of sickness around here and several deaths. Two funerals came through here one day last week, both old ladies that lived down below here. Mr. Jim Moore's mother died last Wednesday. He went to the funeral but Mrs. Moore didn't go.

Well this is Monday morning. I didn't have time to write any last night after I came home from Mrs. Goode's, stayed later than I intended. I found Miss Snapp right nice and pleasant but not near so nice as my sweet Lee. John Hensley and Frank Jackson were there

The restored Aldie Mill as it stands today. The Douglass family owned and operated the mill for six generations since 1834. In 1981 the family donated the mill to the Virginia Outdoors Foundation.

when I got there and old Doctor Metzgar came in soon after I got there. So you see it was quite a crowd of us. Miss Snapp played the organ and we all sang and then we all sat around and let the old Doctor talk to Miss Snapp. Tis cloudy again this morning but hope it won't rain. Write real soon to your loving friend

J. W. B.

TO: Miss E. L. Goode, 39 S. St., N.W., Washington, D.C.

Aldie Va
Apr 29th 1900

My Dearest Lee,

I received your nice, short, sweet letter Friday evening. Had begun to think you wasn't going to write until Sunday but real glad you did write when you did so it gives me a chance to write on Sunday. Went to Sunday School this morning and then to the Presbyterian Church at eleven o'clock. Will go again tonight to hear Mr. Campbell. Have been very lonely this evening, no place to go and most everybody from here gone to Middleburg to Baptist Sunday School Convention. Has been real warm today but is right pleasant now.

When I see your mother I will tell her you don't take much of your time to write to me, that you must write to other people more than to me if you don't have time to write to her. Remember me to them all at home if you find time to write to them. This is Miss Snapp's last Sunday in Aldie unless she comes back again in the fall. School will close next Friday. I don't know what will become of John Hensley after she leaves. He has taken her to Middleburg this evening. Lew and his lady friend have gone too. Hugh and his wife have company today, two of her sisters came up yesterday evening and they all went to Middleburg this morning and have just now come back. I guess you will get a letter from Maude soon, she didn't seem to have your address just right and asked me about it this morning. I told her to be sure and put it N.W. not S.E. so she wrote it in her Sunday School book.

Mr. Vansickler has gone to Leesburg again today but he won't have to go many more times. The ninth of June will soon be here. Mr.

Faulkner was at Mr. Goode's for two or three days this week. You know he is one of Miss Maude's old sweethearts. Suppose Rosa has gone home by this time. If she hasn't and you see her tell her I am real mad at her for not letting us know where she was when I was in city.

Well next Sunday our new preacher will be here and we are all so anxious to see him and to hear him preach. I haven't seen Bob Ogden since I came home but heard he was in Washington last week. Whenever you get ready to come up here let me know a day or two before you come. I haven't sold your buggy yet but I might sell it most anytime now. So you had better come up pretty soon or it will be gone before you come.

This is all I know so will close. Write soon to your loving friend

J. W. B.

TO: Miss E. L. Goode, 39 S St., S.W., Washington, Va

Aldie Va
May 4th 1900

My Dearest Lee

I received your very nice and interesting letter yesterday evening so thought I would try and answer it tonight This being Friday night I don't know if you will get it tomorrow or not but hope you will. I don't know a thing to write so will be like girl at Bush Meeting and say it has been very warm and dusty but is not so very warm tonight. A little fire feels very comfortable.

I saw John Hensley this morning and asked him where he was going Sunday, said he thought he would stay home all day Sunday and rest. I thought maybe he would go to Gainesville as he has a lady friend down there that he hasn't seen for several weeks. I suppose he is at Mrs. Goode's tonight as this is the last night Miss Snapp will be here. She is going to Falls Church tomorrow to spend a few days with Miss Yates before she goes home. She says she is coming back again in the fall but guess she is just joking about coming back for it seems to be the general impression that she will be Mrs. Anderson by that time.

It is very sad about Mr. Davis but no doubt it is much better that they took him away both for him and for the family. Would like ever so well to come down Sunday but feel like it's my place to stay here Sunday when the new preacher comes here for the first time. I haven't heard a word from him though and don't know whether he has come to Middleburg or not. He was to come last week but hadn't come the first of this week. I don't think I have ever told you about Lucy being sick. You remember when I was down there I told you she thought she had whooping cough. So a few days after I came home Mrs. Moore told me she was real sick, had whooping cough and chills. She is better now but not entirely well. Mrs. Moore is going down there tomorrow. She asked me if I wanted to go along with her. I told her I wanted to go bad enough but couldn't go right at this time. I will try and come down one Sunday this month if I can.

I think you are right about going home before you come here though I know all the Aldie people would be glad to see you if you could come but I think you ought to go home whenever you have a chance. I guess if you don't stay in city longer than this month you won't go home until you go to stay. Hope you and Rosa had a nice time at Mr. Tew's, would liked to have been with you. Didn't I tell you what Mr. Faulkner was stopping at Mr. Goode's for? He was down here selling binders and reapers. Mr. Goode is an agent and Mr. Faulkner went around with him and helped him.

I think Miss Jane has gone away again. Saw her go down the road in a buggy with a gentleman from out in the country. I don't know where Miss Maggie Thompson is but it is quite likely she is at Alexandria or wherever she goes down there. Bob told me the last I saw him that she was going down there the first of May. I guess the girls you heard talking about Mr. Bodmer were talking about some other Mr. Bodmer for I don't know but a very few girls in Washington.

Give my love to Ethel next time you see her and tell her I am coming to see her some time. Well I will close for this time. Write soon to your loving friend

John W. B.

Aldie Va
May 11th 1900

My Dear Lee

No doubt you think me slow in answering your last letter and I guess you have a right to. I fully intended writing last night but didn't have an opportunity to do so and so now here it is Friday night again and maybe you won't get this before Monday but maybe you will get it tomorrow evening and then you won't be disappointed. I received your sweet little letter Wednesday evening. Sorry you had such a bad headache Saturday and Sunday and glad I didn't go to see you for I know it would have made it worse for you to be troubled with me you know. I am so tiresome. I did think something about coming next Sunday but have given out the notion for we are busy now. It always spoils me to go to city. I don't feel like work after I come home. I think now I will come on the fourth Sunday, that will be two weeks from next Sunday.

The new preacher preached last Sunday and I think we are all going to like him real well. He seems to be a real nice man. He came down to the house after preaching and stayed a while. Will Bodmer came down with him. There wasn't any of Mr. Goode's folks out to preaching at all. Maude had been away all the week at Halfway and just came home Sunday morning. Had been at her brothers or sisters, I don't know which, helping take care of sick children. Her brother brought her home and then Mrs. Ellison went back with him. I suppose Rosa has gone home by this time but she hasn't written to me yet. I would be real glad to hear from her but I know I could never forget you no matter who came to Aldie. I haven't hardly seen Miss Jane since I was in city, she has been away from home part of the time. I think she has gone away again as I saw her go down the road in a buggy with a gentleman today. I guess you won't hear of our wedding very soon. Maybe I will hear of yours and Uncle George's first. How do Rosa and him get along?

John Hensley didn't stay home last Sunday after all. He went to Gainesville, that is near Haymarket. He has a friend down there, one

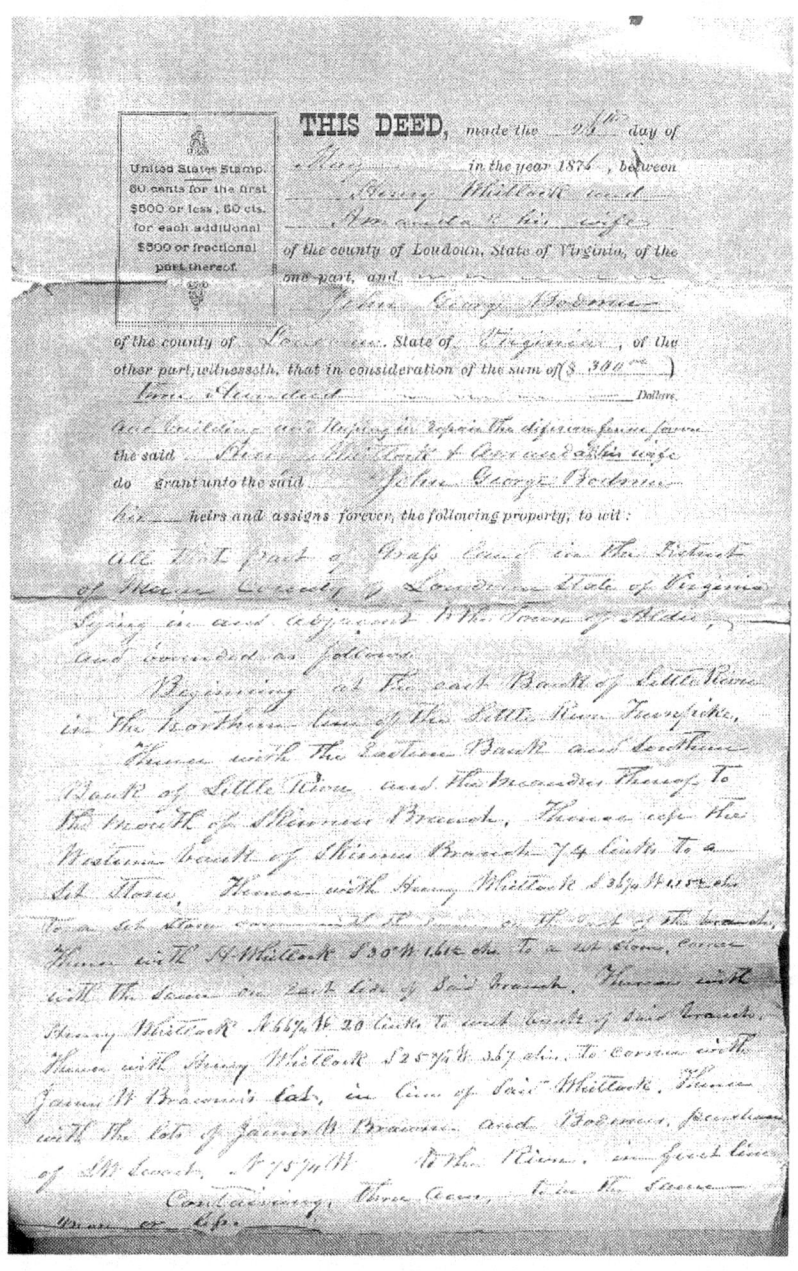

More Bodmer family deeds

And the said _____ Henry Whitlock _____
_____ and Amanda B. his wife _____
covenant that they will warrant generally the property hereby conveyed; that they have the right
to convey the same to the grantee; that the grantee shall have quiet possession thereof, free from all en-
cumbrances, and that they will execute such further assurances of the same, as may be requisite. Witness
the following signatures and seals:

_____ Henry Whitlock _____ {SEAL}

_____ {SEAL}

LOUDOUN COUNTY, to wit:

I, JAMES S. ODEN, a Notary Public for the county aforesaid, in the State of Virginia, do certify that

_____ Henry Whitlock _____

whose name is signed to the writing hereto annexed, bearing date on the __26th__ day of
__May__ , 1876, has acknowledged the same before me, in my county aforesaid.
Given under my hand, this __26th__ day of __May__ , 1876.

_____ James S. Oden _____ N. P.

LOUDOUN COUNTY, to wit:

I, JAMES S. ODEN, a Notary Public for the county aforesaid, in the State of Virginia, do certify
that _____ Amanda B. Whitlock _____ the wife of
_____ Henry Whitlock _____
whose names are signed to the writing hereto annexed, bearing date the __26th__ day of __May__
_____ 1876 , personally appeared before me, in the county aforesaid, and being examined by me privily and apart from her husband, and having the writing aforesaid fully explained to her, she,
the said _____ Amanda B. Whitlock _____ acknowledged the said
writing to be her act, and declared that she had willingly executed the same, and does not wish to retract it.
Given under my hand, this __26th__ day of __May__ , 1876.

_____ James S. Oden _____ N. P.

This Deed,made the 29th.day of January,in the year 1895,be-
-tween John H.Nelson Special Commissioner under the authority
of the decree of Loudoun Circuit Court,made at its January
term 1895,in the Chancery Cause of Thomas vs Neal,of the first
part and George Bodmer,of the second part,witnesseth,that
whereas by decree of Loudoun Circuit Court made at its October
term 1894,in the Chancery suit of Thomas vs Neal,all the real
estate of the late John Neal or Deneal was ordered sold and
by same decree John H.Nelson was appointed a special commis-
to make such sale
-sioner;and whereas said Commissioner after due advertisement
thereof,offered the same at public auction to the highest
bidder on the 10th.day of December 1894,in Leesburg,Va.,and
George Bodmer being the highest bidder became the purchaser
thereof at the price and bid of three hundred dollars;and
whereas by decree made in said cause at the January term 1895,
said sale was confirmed and John H.Nelson was appointed a spe-
-cial commissioner to execute a deed,conveying the real estate,
in the bill and proceedings mentioned,to the said purchaser
when he shall have paid therefor in full,and whereas said
purchaser has paid his purchase money in full and is now en-
-titled to a deed for the said property.

Now therefore this deed witnesseth,that in consideration of
the premises,and the sum of five dollars,the said party of
the first part under the authority of the decree aforesaid
doth hereby grant and convey unto the said party of the second
part his heirs and assigns forever,with special warranty,all
that certain lot or tract of land,situated in Aldie,Loudoun
County,Va.,and is the same recently owned and occupied by the
late John Neal or Deneal,adjoining and bounded by the lands of
W.N.Berkeley,Edmund Tyler and others,on south side of turnpike

and supposed to contain about one acre of land, more or less,
and is the same lot conveyed to said John Neal by C.F. Janney
Commr. by deed recorded in Liber 6 F's folio 243, to which deed
reference is made for greater certainty of description.
Witness the following signature and seal.

Wm. H. Nelson (Seal)

Spec'l Commr.

Clerks office of the County Court of Loudoun County, Virg.
June 20' 1895.

The foregoing deed was this day with me said
office acknowledged by John H. Nelson, Special
Commissioner before me and was admitted to record.

Test, [illegible], clerk

Jno. H. Neal Commr.
to
Geo. Bly &c.

Geo. Bly Plat

1895, January 30"
Received for record this 30th
John H. Nelson
Special Commissioner
to
George Bly, his trustee &c
[illegible] in R. Thompson [illegible] &c
L. 7 F. 235

of Hugh's old sweethearts. Mr. Vansickler and Frank Jackson went to Leesburg. Mr. Vansickler won't have to make many more trips now. He is going Sunday and bring Miss Fannie over here and then Monday he is going to take her down to her home to stay a week or two. He said he don't think he will stop down there just take her and then come right away. I asked him if he wasn't afraid of Mr. Carrington but he said he didn't guess he was very dangerous. I don't know when Lew's friend is going away but guess not before next month. He is at Middleburg this week painting Will Bodmer's house so hasn't had a chance to see her since last Sunday.

Mrs. Moore hasn't come home yet. I don't think Lucy is coming with her but guess she will come up some time during the summer. When is Miss Verge Brawner's wedding to be, this month or next? Well, guess I better close this scribbling and say goodnight. Write real soon to your loving friend

John

TO: *Miss E. L. Goode, 39 S St. N.W., Washington, D.C.*

Aldie Va
May 23rd 1900

My Dear Lee

I will try and write you a short letter but I am not feeling much like writing tonight. I am awfully tired, have worked real hard today and will have to tomorrow and next day. We are very busy, too busy for me to leave for a day. But if nothing happens I am coming to Washington Sunday morning. I may go to Alexandria Saturday evening but will be too late to come to see you for I guess it will be near eight o'clock when the train gets to Alexandria. It leaves Leesburg at 5 minutes after six. I will come to Washington Sunday morning about ten o'clock. I am most afraid to come though for I sold your buggy today.

I haven't seen Miss Jane for the longest time. She is out of town, has been away for quite a while. Oh yes, I will tell you about a call I made Sunday. After preaching John Hensley asked me to go up to Mr. Furr's with him and as I had nothing specially to do of course I went.

There wasn't any other boys there when we got there but we hadn't been there long before a young fellow from up the country came and then pretty soon two more young men from down the country came in and we didn't know how many more were coming so we came home.

I forgot to tell you, I guess I will stay until Monday evening when I come. Mr. Vansickler is talking about going to the city Monday and wants me to stay and come home with him. But he is not sure yet if he is going Monday. Frank Ball and his girl are getting along all right, I guess. He goes to see her every Sunday, rain or shine, and one night during the week. I think Mr. Vansickler is to be married at Mr. Laycock's house. Guess it will be a quiet wedding.

Oh, I almost forgot to tell you about the fire they had in Purcellville, but guess you will hear about it before you get this. Mr. Pancoart's store and the town hall, lumber yard, drug store and several other buildings were burned. I think it happened last night but I just heard it this evening.

Well you may expect me Sunday morning. I will be there if the trains don't stop running before that time. From your loving friend

J. W. B.

TO: *Miss E. L. Goode, 39 S St., N.W., Washington, D.C.*

Aldie Va
June 3rd 1900

My Dearest Lee

I was certainly delighted to receive your nice letter yesterday evening, had been thinking that maybe you wouldn't have time to write until today and that would have seemed an awful long time to wait.

I saw Maude at Sunday School this morning. She wanted to know if you sent a message by me. I couldn't think of anything you had told me to tell her. She said I was a bad boy to go off to the city without telling her anything about it. I'm awfully sorry they didn't know I was going but I thought Mr. Goode would surely tell them.

We had a new preacher to preach for us this afternoon, Mr. Bain from Gainesville. He preached at Middleburg this morning and yesterday morning. Dr. Boyd couldn't come so sent Mr. Bain in his place and Mr. Sutton went down to Gainesville today to preach in Mr. Bain's place.

I did not get off to go to Middleburg yesterday, thought I would come right straight home after services but Will Bodmer insisted that I stay to dinner and then by that time it looked so much like rain, and you know I don't like to start any place when it looks like rain. So I waited until after the rain was over and didn't get home until after five o'clock. We had a real nice rain and today is a little cooler. Frank is much better, was at the shop yesterday. Mr. Vansickler didn't go to Leesburg today, went down the country to see his little girl. His time is getting short but he seems to be in a hurry for the day to come. Certainly it would be all right for you to go to the depot to see them. I believe I told you before what train they were going on, leave Leesburg at 6:05 and I guess get to city about half past 7.

Tom went out to Halfway this evening, think this the first time he has been out there since last fall. John Hensley I guess has gone to Gainesville. I saw him pass by here this morning. I went to the festival at Episcopal Church Friday night but didn't stay long. Wasn't very many there. The Presbyterians are going to have theirs next Thursday night. The Douglass girls came home from school yesterday.

I haven't heard a word about Miss Jane since I came home so don't know when she will be home. She has been away quite a while. We are going to start the Young People's Prayer Meeting again tonight. Will be at Presbyterian Church. Guess will keep it up now until winter. Mr. Vansickler isn't going to stay in the city very long. I think they are coming home Friday on train that gets to Leesburg at 3 o'clock. Guess they will get a good serenade. Some of the boys told him last night that they were going to serenade him.

I don't believe I told you that Mr. Faulkner was here again last week. Stayed from Monday until Thursday morning. Seems to like to come to Aldie for some reason. Well it is most time to go to prayer meeting so will say goodbye. Write real soon to your loving friend

John

Aldie Va
June 5th 190C

My Dear Lee

I know you will be surprised to hear from me so soon again but the ladies of the Methodist Church are going to hold a strawberry festival next Tuesday evening and Mrs. Goode was down town this evening and stopped to see me and asked if I thought you would come up at that time. She said she would write to you herself but was afraid you wouldn't answer her letter right away. So she asked me to write to you and see if you couldn't come. She was just joking about you not answering her letter but told me to tell you anyhow. I think it would be awfully nice if you could come and I know all the people up here would be glad to see you and I would just be delighted. I will meet you at Leesburg any time you come. If you can't come any sooner you could come up Tuesday morning or evening on 3 o'clock train but would be better to come in morning and then if you can't stay any longer you can go back next evening. Let me know as soon as you can if you are coming. Well Goodnight, it is after ten o'clock. From your loving friend

John

Aldie Va
June 13th 190J

My Dear Lee

I guess you are thinking that I won't write you as many letters as I did last week and I expect you will think right for here it is Wednesday night already but it hasn't been so I could write any sooner. Guess I can't write very much now. Monday night I was feeling very badly, had a real bad headache all day so didn't feel like writing or doing anything else. Last night I was at the festival until nearly twelve o'clock so couldn't write then. It was too bad that it rained last night and spoiled the festival but still we had quite a nice time if there wasn't very many there. It was at the school house and we had plenty of room but it would have been so nice out of doors if it hadn't rained. They did have three or four tables out in the yard until there came up another shower. It rained in the evening just about time the festival started so had to move in schoolhouse. Then it stopped raining and moved outdoors again and then it rained again so had to move back in doors again. Miss Jane wasn't there, she intended to come but the lady she is nursing was taken worse again yesterday morning so she couldn't come. Miss Maude was there and looked real nice, told me she had a letter from you Monday. So you did write to her real soon. I haven't seen Mrs. Goode since last week. I told Maude you would come up before you go to Ellicott City but she said you never said a word about coming in her letter. She said they were all very sorry you couldn't come to the festival but said maybe when you did come you could stay a while.

I saw in the paper Saturday that it was to be Children's Day services at Mt. Vernon Sunday and wished I could go, hope you went and enjoyed it. Most everybody is getting ready to go to the Upperville Horse Show tomorrow but it looks now as if it might be a rainy day. Some went today, Mr. and Mrs. Vansickler and Frank Ball and a few others. I think most everybody but myself are going tomorrow but I never cared to go. Mr. Faulkner was here again yesterday and today and was at the festival last night. I didn't see him talking to Maude any though. I haven't heard a word about Camp meeting, so I don't know what they are going to do, only know it is going to be about same time as last year so you had better hurry or you might not get home by that time. But as I told you last summer it don't make any difference if you stay in the city all the summer. I know it was warm down there Monday and Tuesday. I saw in the paper one day last week that Olla Haley was married in Washington.

Guess I had better close for this time as I am getting sleepy and have written about all I know anyway. You must excuse this bad writing. Don't know if you will be able to read it or not. If you can't just guess at it. Write real soon to your loving friend

John

P.S. Haven't got that letter from Rosa yet. J.

The dam at Aldie

TO: Miss Lee Goode, #39 S St., North West, Washington, D.C.

Bailey's Cross Rds
June 19, 1900

My Very Dear Lee

No doubt from my long silence you think I have taken rooms over to St. Elizabeth's. Cannot say I blame you for thinking otherwise. Just to think two Sundays passed, your kind invitation not acknowledged yet. I should certainly hide myself in some secluded place. If I am going contrary to my promise all the time, it seems to me like I have so many engagements usually on Sundays I cannot run in to see you at all. My friend whom I am visiting said to me to invite you out to spend just as much time as you could. I thought now if you have not gone home, on your way up home you could stop and spend a few days. I will meet you at Glen Carlin the second Sta out from Washington. Now will you not do this? If you are still in the City? Write soon as you get this.

I am going in to the City on Friday of this week to see something in regards to getting employment of some kind. It seems to me I am hardly in my right mind. My dear, it's so hard to be disappointed in a person, especially in the way I have been. I hope not one of my friends will ever have to go through the same I have for death is Preferable.

Now I am not going to write any more than a note comparatively what I might write. Write to me soon as you get this.

With fondest Love, Sincerely Your Friend

Marguerite

TO: *Miss E. L. Goode, Purcellville, Va*

Aldie Va
July 24th 1900

My Dearest Lee

Well I don't know very much to write but will write a little bit anyway. It seems like most everybody has gone out of Aldie since you and Miss Jane left. I just feel lost now of nights. It seems so strange for me not to go uptown. Last night it was rainy. We had a real hard rain so I lay down and the first thing I knew Lew was calling me and I got up it was most ten o'clock. So I went to bed. It hasn't been quite so warm today and we had a little shower this evening and it is real pleasant tonight.

Hugh came back from Haymarket early yesterday morning. Left his old lady down there to go to the Horse Show. Mr. and Mrs. Vansickler went yesterday evening. I saw Eddie Watson yesterday and today both. Says he is going to Purcellville next week to see you as he didn't get to see you while you were here.

There was a very sudden death about 3 miles below here yesterday. A young man named Wilson. He had been in poor health for quite a while but was feeling no worse than usual. He lay down yesterday like he had been in the habit of doing and when they called him to dinner they found him dead. Had just gone to sleep and never waked up.

I know you will have trouble reading this but if you can't make it out I will read it for you next week. Give my love to all home and write soon to your loving friend

John

Aldie Va
July 29th, 19C0

My Dear Lee,

I have kept putting off writing all day and now I can't put it off any longer as it is now after 9 o'clock. I have just come from church. Mr. Campbell preached this morning and again tonight. There wasn't any preaching at either of the other churches. I kind of looked for a letter from you Saturday but it didn't come. I received your nice short letter all right Wednesday evening. Real glad you got home al right. I thought maybe you would have to stay in Purcellville Monday night after the storm came up. It rained every day after you went home until Thursday and then it rained most all day. It looks now as if it might rain again soon. Hope it will tomorrow so there won't be any dust for Bush Meeting. I will be up Wednesday morning and won't stop at the grounds but will come right on to your house if it isn't rainy. If it is raining I guess I won't come until Saturday evening.

I think Rosa must like the city—if she has gone back again. Guess her and Uncle George will come up Wednesday. I saw the old doctor today. Said he had been up to see you and you told him to tell me it wouldn't be worth while for me to come any more. I told him I thought I would go once more any way. Haven't seen Maudie to speak to her since you left. Will say Goodbye until I see you.

Lovingly,

John

Aldie Va
Aug 7th 1900

My Dear Lee

The weather has been something awful today but is getting right pleasant now out of doors. But is very warm in the house where there is a lamp but I guess I can stand to do a little writing anyway. We got home all right Sunday night but it was most twelve o'clock when we got here. It was real cool driving and Harry went to sleep several times on the way. I haven't told anybody what time it was when we came and you mustn't tell either. We got home before John Hensley did though. It was twelve when he got home. I didn't get up very early next morning but didn't feel sleepy during the day and didn't sleep very well last night.

The boys have been getting ready for Camp meeting today. Have had quite a time getting everything ready. They are going to move up tomorrow and finish fixing up so that they will be ready by Friday. There was a preacher and his family went through here today on the way to Camp meeting. They came from over in Maryland. I think they will be in time. I was up on the bridge for a while after supper tonight and Miss Jane came by but she was in a hurry and didn't hardly have time to spend. I would have gone up the street with her but was too tired. I hope it won't be so warm tomorrow. It has really been too warm today to work and we have quite a good deal of work on hand.

I don't believe I told you about Gene on Sunday. You know he was at Bush meeting Wednesday and came home that night and went on up to his home. Next day he went down by here and came back Friday evening late and then he came down Saturday to bring the buggy home but didn't come to work until Monday morning. Mr. Jackson was real mad at him for staying away so long.

I heard some good news today. Lucy is at the Plains and will come back with Mrs. Moore when she comes home. Mr. Moore didn't go up the country. He had a good deal of work on hand and thought he had best stay home. He is going up Saturday and bring them all back Monday if he can get a horse to go. I expect I will go to Camp meeting Sunday but it seems that none of the rest want to go if it stays as warm as it has been for the last two days. Hope you will have some way to go for would be so lonely for me without you.

Well this is all I know to write so will have to close. Trusting to hear from you real soon. I am as ever your loving

John

Aldie Va
Aug 13th 1900

My Dearest Lee

I don't hardly know what to write but guess the first thing I had better tell you is that Lucy is here at last but I haven't seen her yet. Would have gone over a little while tonight but didn't have time to go over there and write to you both so thought I had better write to you. I believe I would rather write to you than to talk to her. There is a young lady from Alexandria visiting at Mr. Wrenn's, came Sunday. I haven't seen her either.

I suppose you didn't get to Camp Meeting yesterday. I didn't see anything of you. Saw Perry and Clarence Davis, just caught a glimpse of Perry in the morning and thought I would see him again but never saw him again the whole day. You may be glad you were not there for it wasn't a bit of pleasure. The dust was just awful. I think worse than I ever saw it. Guess it was nice today though, There was a good rain up there yesterday evening and there was quite a wind storm but didn't do very much damage, just blew part of the roof off two or three of the tents. The boys were awfully scared about their tent but didn't do them any damage. They are doing real well so far but can't tell yet how they will come out. Miss Lillie is boarding on the grounds with Mr. Chas Monroe, but think she spends most of her time with Hugh and the other boys.

John Hensley's girl was there yesterday and took supper with the boys. I didn't see anything of Verge. If you see her tell her I looked for her all day. Saw one of those Middleburg girls, the one that was at Bush Meeting. Her two sisters are away from home. I didn't have much chance to talk to her for she had a fellow with her all day long, only a short while in the morning she was alone. I don't know if I will go any more before Sunday or not. We are so busy I don't like to lose the time to go. I only heard one sermon yesterday, Dr. Leftwick from Tennessee. He is a real good speaker but hasn't a very strong voice and people in the back part of the tent can't hear him very well.

I suppose Mrs. Murray has gone by now. Guess you miss the little boy little as Miss Maude called him. I haven't seen Maude since we came from Bush Meeting. Don't know if she is going to Camp Meeting or not but expect some of them will go next Sunday if it is a good day. I hope it will be so you all can come next Sunday. That will be the biggest day if it don't get dusty again by that time. We didn't have any rain here yesterday, only a little sprinkle. Gene took Miss Fry up yesterday and today he and another boy from Middleburg went to Leesburg to August Court. I guess I better stop for this time. Write soon to your loving

John

TO: *Miss E. L. Goode, Purcellville, Va*

Aldie Va
Aug 21st 1900

My Dearest Lee

Well I can't go to see Lucy tonight so will write to you. Lew came home today and has gone over to see Lucy so I thought I had better stay home tonight. I was just over there last night and when Lucy saw me coming she wanted to know if I felt lonely. I told her yes and that was the reason I came to see her, that I only come to see her when I don't have any other place to go.

I expect I got home most as soon as you did Sunday. We started about six o'clock and got home before eight. We started just after Mr. Moore but they stopped at Mr. Hall's a few minutes and we passed them there. Was a good many carriages and buggies on the road and we got a good dusting. We had a real nice rain last night and has been cloudy most all day today and is beginning to rain again now. Guess we will have plenty of rain now that Camp meeting is over. They have decided to hold the Camp meeting again next year. I didn't hardly think they would break it up. It would seem so strange not to have it. We are all so used to going every summer. The boys are all very tired. Say they are glad it is over. I haven't heard them say just how much they made but think they did right well.

I haven't seen Maude since Sunday and haven't heard if Mr. and Mrs. Goode are going up to see you or not. If they go I don't expect I will but if they don't go I guess I can come up Saturday evening. You must excuse the paper I have been using lately. I never think to get any, only when I go to write. Frank Jackson left the Camp Grounds about the same time that Miss Maude and the children started. Guess he didn't care to bring you to Aldie after I told him he would have to take you home again. Well I don't know anything else to write so will have to close. Write soon to your loving friend

John

TO: *Miss E. L. Goode, Purcellville, Va. Loudoun County*

(postmarked SEP 10, 1900
Aldie, Va.)

My dear Miss Goode,

Mr. Ogden is able to go to office but I've been quite ill myself. Now am feeling better so if you will let me know when it will be convenient for you to come to us shall be much obliged as I am quite anxious to have a little sewing done we are in need of.

Yours in haste

J. E. Ogden
Wednesday Eve

No envelope

Aldie Va
Sept 10th 1900

My Dearest Lee

I don't know if you are disappointed today or not but I know I am. I surely did want to come up to see you today but couldn't get a horse anywhere. Frank took Alice home this morning and used Dolly so I couldn't get her. I thought I could get Mr. Goode's horse but Mr. Vansickler used her. Then I thought of Mr. Jackson's horse and found that Frank Jackson was going to Leesburg and he had to have a horse. I guess though it is as well that I had to stay home for it is too warm to go anywhere today and I told you I wouldn't come again until the weather was cooler. I didn't expect that I would want to come up today the first part of the week. I thought that Mr. and Mrs. Goode were going up to Purcellville and to your house. They said they were going all the week until the last of the week and then Mr. Goode got out of the notion of going. Guess they won't go next week either for the school teachers are coming Saturday or Sunday and are going to board there. I think Mr. and Mrs. Vansickler are going to board there the balance of the year. Don't know why they are going to leave Mr. Jerega's.

Miss Jane was at Sunday School this morning and seemed in a real good humor. After Sunday School she told me she expected to be at Mrs. Goode's tonight and asked me to come up, so guess I will have to go. Rachel Palmer has gone to spend a few days with Miss Maggie Thompson. She and another young lady came up last Friday and Rachel went home with them. I went to Little River Church this morning after Sunday School. Had no idea of going, was sitting on porch and Gus Jerega came along in his buggy and asked me to go with him. I hadn't been there to preaching for two years and enjoyed the drive and the sermon very much.

Where is Sam Ellmore to be married? Guess you will go to the wedding. Tom went to Leesburg with Frank Jackson this afternoon. Guess he has found a girl over there. I don't believe I told you about Lew's lady friend from Washington being at Mr. Gulick's for a few days. She came one day last week and stayed until Monday morning. She is not coming to teach Mr. Gulick's children this year so guess Lew will have to go to the city once in a while to see her.

I don't know when I can come up now but will come just as soon as I possibly can. It seems so long since I saw you. If I can come next Sunday I will let you know the last of the week. I don't like to leave here next Sunday. It is preaching day at our church and Communion day but I want to see you and expect I will miss preaching. I do hope it will turn cooler this week for it has really been too warm to work. We are still right busy in the shop.

I did go to see Maude last Sunday night. Found Mr. Jackson there but he left soon after I got there. I only stayed until nine o'clock. I am glad to know that Mr. Davis was well enough to come home with the boys and hope he will continue to improve.

Sorry to hear of so much fever in Purcellville. I guess you miss the two young men since they left but suppose you still have Frank Tew

George Bodmer

with you. Well I have written out so will close. Write real soon to your loving

John

Aldie Va
Sept 19th 1900

My Dearest Lee

My time is short tonight so will only write a very short letter. I received your nice letter yesterday evening and thought I would answer it right away but didn't have time to do so. I expected you would give me a good scolding but was very agreeably surprised when I read your letter. We were disappointed Sunday about preaching.

The preacher didn't come, it was so rainy Saturday that he thought it would rain all day Sunday and so he didn't come. Mr. Sutton didn't like it a bit.

I will be up Sunday and will start from here about half past ten so will get there not later than two o'clock and maybe sooner. I don't like to miss Sunday School or I could come Saturday. The weather is so nice and cool now but we haven't had much rain yet. Had a right nice rain Saturday but seems as dry as ever again. Miss Jane has left Aldie again, is at Mr. Lewis's nursing his daughter who has typhoid fever. I guess you won't hardly go to work this week as tomorrow is the twentieth and then there are only two more days in this week.

Mr. Moore is going to move to Rectortown. He was up there and rented a place last week. Mrs. Hugh Bruin has gone to Baltimore, went Monday. I guess the school teachers will come Saturday or Sunday as school begins next Monday. Well if I don't hear from you I will be up Sunday and tell you all the news. With love to all I am as ever your loving friend

John

TO: Miss Ella Goode, Purcellville, Loudoun Co, Va

GOOD BROTHERS,
DEALERS IN
General Merchandise,
SHIPPING POINT:
Stone's Wharf._____   St. Mary's County.

Bryantown, Md
Sept 25 1900

My Dear Lee

I will today take this chance to write you to answer your letter. I intended to answer your letter last week but was sick with the pneuralgia and still have it yet. I hope this may find you well and enjoying good health. Well I guess you are in Leesburg by this time. I expect to go to the city this week if I can get off.

You wanted to know when I was going to marry—I don't know. Sometime between the first of next month and the middle. The young lady has gotten here but is sick in bed now. Am very afraid she has the typhoid fever. You wanted to know her name. Mollie Gray is the name. They are nice people. The young lady is making her clothes and would like for you to come down to see us Xmas if you can. If you say you cannot, write to me. You wanted to know about Rosa and Bruce. They have fallen out for good. I heard down home when I was there. I am going down home Monday and come back Tuesday. I have never heard from Maurice since Rose's death.

Well Lee, my dear girl, I cannot write much today. I have the neuralgia so bad and will promise to do better next time. I want to go to see my girl today if I can get off but I don't have much chance to do anything.

You wanted to know where I was going to marry. I will marry here on account of expenses. She is a Catholic. The church is about a half a mile from the village. Well I must stop. Don't think I don't want to write by making my letter short. I am feeling bad. By By with love and kisses. I still remain your true friend

Cousin Geo

TO: Miss E. L. Goode, Purcellville, Loudoun County, Va.

Aldie Va.
Sept, 25th 1900

My Dearest Lee,

I didn't get home last night until nearly eight o'clock and it was real dark. Was about sundown when I got to Philomont and before I got through the woods at Goose Creek it had gotten quite dark, but I wasn't afraid. They all say I came home mad and that I have been mad all day today. But I haven't been mad at all. I did get a little worried at Frank about going hunting yesterday and leaving George all alone in the shop. He thought I would be home in the morning and went squirrel hunting with Lew. They had right good luck. Lew killed eleven squirrels and Frank eight. It seems as if I never can stay away a day unless something goes wrong and I have been scolding myself

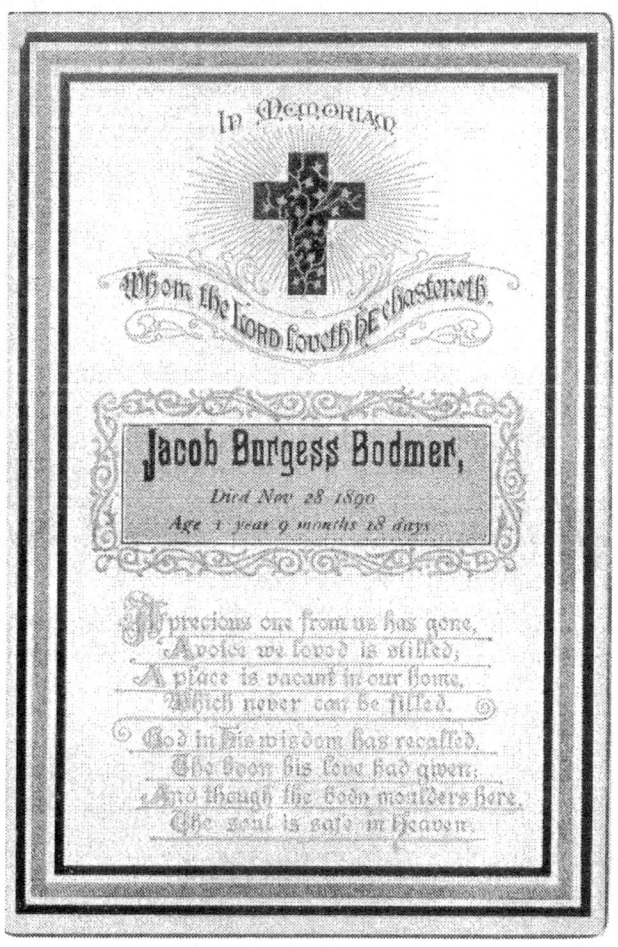

In Memoriam

Whom the Lord loveth He chasteneth

Jacob Burgess Bodmer,
Died Nov 28 1890
Age 1 year 9 months 18 days

A precious one from us has gone,
A voice we loved is stilled;
A place is vacant in our home,
Which never can be filled.

God in His wisdom has recalled
The boon his love had given,
And though the body moulders here,
The soul is safe in Heaven.

all day today for not coming home in the morning as I had intended. Frank seems to be getting so stubborn. Says I ought to stay home myself so guess I will have to do as he says. When I go away Saturday evenings and stay Sunday he won't go to Sunday School. Says it's my place to be there. Guess I will have to stay home all the time he is.

I gave Mr. Goode the strap, guess he took it to Mrs. Goode alright. I haven't seen any of the rest of them. Gene has been away since Sunday. He told me last week he wanted to get off Monday and Tuesday but I thought he was just joking. I don't know where he has gone but think he went somewhere down in Fairfax. Miss Jane came home last night and Mrs. Marshall Carter has gone to Mr. Lewis's in her place. Don't know why she came home but guess she wanted to rest a while before she goes to the Asylum. I think she expects to go about the first of next month.

The children all seem to like the new teacher real well. There are several boys that are a good deal larger than he is. I guess I can't come up next Sunday. Would like to but think I had better not. Will try and see you soon though. Hugh and Miss Lillie haven't come home yet but think they intend to come tonight. Now you must write to me real soon. Hope you have gotten in a good humor by this time. With love to all I am as ever your own true, loving

John

TO: Miss E. L. Goode, Purcellville, Va

Aldie Va
Sept 27th 1900

My Dear Lee

I received your nice letter yesterday evening and was a little surprised but very glad to hear from you so soon. We both wrote at the same time. I wonder if we are both writing at same time tonight. We had a real nice shower tonight and looks as if it might rain again tonight. It has been real warm for a few days. Hope it will be cooler tomorrow. I have worked right hard all week but have been a day behind, every day seeming like it was one day earlier in the week than it was. Today has seemed just like it was Wednesday. It will soon be Sunday again and I would love to see you but think it best for me to stay home next Sunday.

I do hope you won't have to go to Washington, think it would be so much nicer in Leesburg. There is going to be a big time at Methodist Church in Leesburg from 9th to 12th of October. It is Epworth League and Missionary Convention. Guess it will be real nice and then the next week there is to be revival services. Hugh and his wife came home Wednesday morning. He asked me to guess who he saw in Washington and I told him I guessed Rosa. He said that was who it was and she looked real nice. Guess I will get a whipping when

I see Mrs. Goode. She told Frank she was going to whip me as soon as she saw me for not letting her know I was going to Purcellville last Sunday. Guess I ought to have told them but thought it wouldn't make any difference. I didn't see anybody when I went by the house. Lew has been writing a letter tonight so I waited until he got through. He was an awful long time. Guess he knew more to write than I do. Miss Jane was downtown this afternoon. First time I had seen her for some time. The new school teacher seems to be very attentive to Miss Snapp. Whenever you see her he is always with her. Maybe he ain't so hard to catch.

Well I reckon I had better close for this time. Write real soon to your true loving friend

J. W. B.

John W. Bodmer
and
Ella Lee Goode were married
January 17th, 1901
in Washington, D.C.

❧ Later Years

FR.: Chas S. Stanton, Pastor
Methodist Episcopal Church
South, Clifton Forge, Virginia

March 15, 1904

Dear John,

Your letter, which I received this morning, was quite a welcome surprise. I had heard from you only in the most indirect way for so long, and heard so little even then, that I would probably have been in danger of forgetting you, but for the daily reminder of the Bodmer handiwork in my book case, which is always in sight as I sit in my study. It is quite a great comfort, especially just now, as I know I shall have to pack up within a month, and know that all the packing the books need is to screw the tops on the boxes, and they are ready to go to the freight office.

You handle larger and stronger tools so regularly that I guess you find it too small a business to try to grip so small and slender a tool as a pen, and this accounts for your abstinence from it. However, I appreciate very much your finally taking it into your head to write me, for it disproves, in my case at least, an old adage, "out of sight out of mind."

I knew you were married, but was surprised to reflect that it has been three years since the happy intelligence reached me. How the years fly past, and how soon we grow old. We scarcely begin to live before we begin to decay. I am not real sure I have met Mrs. Bodmer, before she became such, but, of course I feel an interest in all that concerns her, because of her intimate relationship to you. By this time she knows just how badly she was fooled when she listened to your soft talk, but it's too late to do her any good now. She'll just have to grin and bear it.

It is not very easy for me to associate you in my mind with two children of your own. When I knew you you would have been somewhat afraid of a baby. You were apparently such a confirmed old bachelor that not even the most trustful of mothers would have risked her baby with you for even an hour, without feeling certain that something dreadful would happen to you and to the baby before she got back. The little tots, with all their helplessness and innocence, come into our homes without a rag to their backs, but somehow they wrap themselves around our hearts in a way that makes us better for having them, and for having loved them. They are lots of trouble and worry, but they are worth it all, and more. I know the little girls are an attraction and a comfort, not only to you, but to the grandparents as well.

Yes, I am shaping up for the end of the year. I shall start for Alexandria two weeks from today, if nothing happens to interfere with my calculations. I shall not come back here, of course. For many reasons I am sorry it is so. While this has been the hardest work I have ever had, it has been, on the whole, the most pleasant. The fellow who serves this work eats no idle bread, and works day and night, as regularly as a doctor.

First of all, we are at the end of three divisions of the C & O. One division begins here, and runs west, and there are two east—one across the mountains to Charlottesville, Gordonsville and Richmond and Washington, and the other follows the banks of the James River to Lynchburg and Richmond. The road changes from eastern to central time here, and this makes it necessary for all train crews to change when the train reaches here. This means a great deal when you remember that one thousand train men run into and out of Clifton Forge. This includes only engineers, firemen, brakemen, and baggage men, flag men, conductors and porters. Express messengers and mail agents are additional to these. It is a little confusing to a stranger to find two sets of time. For instance a Washington train arrives here from Cincinnati every morning at 8 o'clock, stays only ten minutes, and leaves at 9-10. But stranger still, the train from Washington to Cincinnati arrives here at 6-28 in the morning, stays ten minutes, and leaves at 5-38. The night train arrives at 9-15 p m, and leaves at 8-25, after spending ten minutes here. While this is very confusing to a stranger, it is as plain and natural as anything else after one gets used to it. The men who run west from here have their watches just one hour slower than those who run east, and when a fellow talks about time, it is usually qualified by the phrases "fast time" or "slow time"; but as often by the equally expressive "your time" or "our time".

186 🎔

The round house, repair shops, and wrecking forces are located here because it is a central location, and in these departments about 700 or 1,000 more men are employed. Then the division offices are located here and the officials and their clerks and messengers and another contingent to the railroad forces.

Of course the life of a railroad man is very irregular. He has no regular time to do anything, but goes when he is called, comes home when he can, and sleeps and eats whenever he gets a chance. To keep in touch with them is no small task, and if the preacher does not keep in touch with them they let him and his services alone. It keeps a fellow all the time chasing around to look them up and keep them interested in religious work. It takes grace and much ginger in the heels.

Of course a railroad cannot be run without accidents. Some of them are always being hurt or killed, and when anything happens, they call the preacher out just as they are called. We all have telephones in our parsonages, and our central office runs night and day, so we are called any time they want us. The hospital is about a mile and a half from the parsonage, and it is not easy to get out some sleety, stormy or snowy night, dress in a hurry, and sail out at 2 or 3 o'clock in the morning.

Then people are always moving in and out, and if a fellow does not find them out and get them into his church, they soon drift off. And in a few years enough of his regular congregation has left town to leave him only a fragment of a congregation. You may imagine what this moving amounts to when I tell you that of the 270 members I have now, I have taken in 160 and still I have hardly a dozen more members now than I had when I came here. Of 9 stewards, only two of those here when I came are still members of the board, and I guess we have had twenty different men in the four years.

Still, the people are very kind. I have gotten intimately acquainted with the officials, and get a pass on the road whenever I want it. I took the whole family last fall on a trip to Hinton, Huntington, Ceredo, Central City and Kenova, W. Va., and Catlettsburg and Ashland in Kentucky, on a pass good for sixty days. The trip cost us only hotel and street car fares. This has enabled me to take a number of trips I could not otherwise have taken, and I appreciate it all the more because no other preacher gets passes here, not even the pastors of the officials. But I earn all I get, I can assure you.

My own members are very appreciative and kind. They have raised my salary from $800 to $900, gave me a suit of clothes each

Christmas since I have been here, and show us many other tokens of kindness.

They built us a bathroom, put in a $65 range in the kitchen, with forty gallon hot water tank, and geared this to a bathroom with marble top wash stand, and porcelain lined bath tub, and porcelain stool. We have one of the best and most convenient parsonages in the Conference.

While I shall be sorry to leave all these, still, I am convinced that our four year limit is wisest, and I am sure it will be better for them and for me that I should go, even if I get a less desirable place.

Of course I have no idea where I will go, but I guess I will get as good a place as I deserve. I am like the man though, who was in court to be tried on an indictment. He seemed so scared that somebody went to him and said, "O, I wouldn't be scared, you'll get justice done you here." He responded, "Faith, and it's just that I'm afeard of."

I should be glad indeed to pay you a visit, as you are kind enough to invite me to do, but I cannot spend the Sunday of Conference with you at Aldie. First of all, I sadly need to hear a sermon occasionally. I rarely have the opportunity to hear anybody preach and if I did not take advantage of every opportunity to hear one, I should soon be in danger of backsliding. I want very much to hear the sermons at conference on Sunday.

Then, I have promised a steward here, who has never been either to Washington or Baltimore, to take him over to Baltimore Saturday afternoon, and if we go there we shall not get back to Alexandria

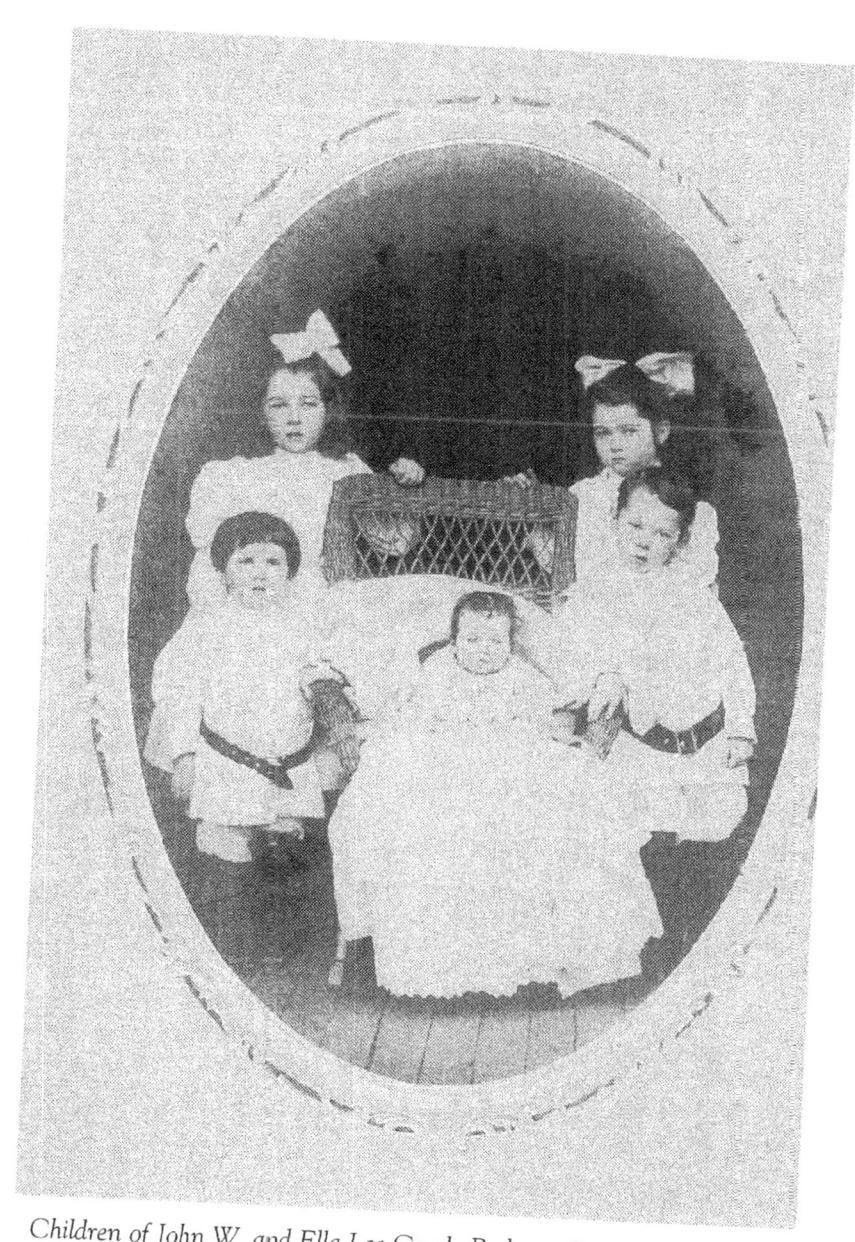

Children of John W. and Ella Lee Goode Bodmer. From top left clock-wise: Margaret, Helen, Gordon, baby Virginia, and John Perry

until very late. I guess he will have his wife with him, and I promised him long I ago I would take him over.

It is just possible that I could run in for a night after Conference, but that will depend on where I am sent, and I cannot tell about it until the appointments are read out. But if I can make it suit to come up and see you, even for a little while, I shall be delighted to do so. I have only the most pleasant recollections of association with you, and would be glad to look into your face again, and especially glad to make the acquaintance of the little Bodmer girls.

You will remember me kindly to all the friends I may still have in Aldie, and especially to your folks at home. I have made a good many errors in this, but it is because I am breaking in a new machine. It is a little stiff in the joints, as yet, and it is this that gives it the disposition to stammer and swear occasionally, instead of writing along smoothly and religiously. I am glad to know Bro. Kuhlman is in favor among you, and trust you have had a good year in all the work of the church, and in your own business as well. And now that you have worn the rust off your pen, use it again soon in writing me another letter. I am sincerely your friend,

Chas. S. Stanton

John and Ella Lee Bodmer and family at home in Aldie

Margaret's report card

Ella Lee Goode Bodmer

Aerial view of the home of John and Ella Lee Bodmer in Aldie

JOHN W. BODMER
Wheelwright
Dealer in Vehicles
Aldie, Va.

No.

LEESBURG

Pay TO THE

JOHN W. BODMER
Wheelwright
Dealer in Vehicles
Aldie, Va.

No.

LEESBURG, VA., Sept. 23rd 1910

Pay TO THE
ORDER OF T. E. Bodmer $40.00

Forty   DOLLARS

For

THE LOUDOUN NATIONAL

JOHN W. BODMER
Wheelwright
Dealer in Vehicles
Aldie, Va.

No.

LEESBURG, VA., Sept. 23 191_

$40

Pay TO THE
ORDER OF T. E. Bodmer   DOLLARS

Forty

For

THE LOUDOUN NATIONAL BANK,
LEESBURG, VA.

No.

191_

$

THE LOUDOUN NATIONAL BANK,
LEESBURG, VA.

DOLLARS

Pay TO THE
ORDER OF Dr. E. G. Eliot   LEESBURG, VA., Jan 1st

For   1912

$20.00/100

THE LOUDOUN NATIONAL BANK
LEESBURG, VA.

DOLLARS

For

THE LOUDOUN NATIONAL BANK
LEESBURG, VA.

JOHN W. BODMER
Wheelwright
Dealer in Vehicles
Aldie, Va.

No.

LEESBURG, VA., Oct. 24th 1910

JOHN W. BODMER
Wheelwright
Dealer in Vehicles
Aldie, Va.

No.

LEESBURG, VA., Oct. 2_th 1911

Pay TO THE
ORDER OF George Bodmer $5.52/100

Five & 52/100   DOLLARS

For

THE LOUDOUN NATIONAL BANK,

John W. Bodmer, 1929

Postcards sent to Margaret Settle Goode the last year of her life

Scene near PURCELLVILLE, VA.

Family Trees

Goode Family

GOODE DESCENDANCY

Roswell Goode was born ca 1758, died between Sept. and Dec. 1808. He lived in Trinity Parish, Charles County, Md. He took the oath of allegiance and served in Captain Clarkson's Company as a private in the Revolutionary War in 1778 (Bryantown 100, Md.)

> Records of Proof—Roswell Goode 4th gen.—Will probated 12/13/1808
> Will Book HB BH Liber 13, Folio 13
> Patriot Oath of Fidelity Charles Co., Md.
> See No. 467730 DAR for source
> Blue Book No. 5, Folio 30, Hall of Records, Annapolis
> Brambaugh, Vol 1, page 311
> DAR National No 467730—Mrs. Gertrude Stambaugh
> Unpublished Revolutionary Records of Md. Vol. 2, p. 245

1 Roswell GOODE b: ABT 1752 Charles Co., MD; d: Ryceville family farm, Charles County MD
+ Elizabeth HAYDEN b: ABT 1762 d: 23 Mar 1832
  *2 Peregrine GOODE b: 7 SEP 1799 Charles Co., MD d: After 1861 Charles Co. MD
   + Ellen CARTWRIGHT b: ABT 1822 St. Mary's Co., MD d: 8 Sep 1851
     3 Thomas William GOODE b: 2/11/1841
     + Elisabeth SINE
     3 Lucinda A. GOODE b: 9/1844
     + Kingsley DAVIS
     3 James Henry GOODE b: 2/9/1846
     + 1. Ellen TURNER
        2. Rebecca H. COPSEY
  ** 3 Samuel Perry GOODE b: 8 Sep 1850 St. Mary's Co., MD
     d: 5 Aug 1892 Loudoun Co., VA
    + Margaret C SETTLE b: 28 May 1852 Loudoun Co., VA
     d: 13 Sep 1925 Aldie, VA
   ***4 Ella Lee GOODE b: 16 AUG 1874 d: 10 JUN 1952
     m: 17 JAN 1901
     + John W BODMER b: 30 AUG 1868 d: 2 FEB 1944
       5 Margaret BODMER b: 16 NOV 1901 d: 4 FEB 1986
       + Paul Edward ALBAUGH b: 11 JUN 1905 d: 29 SEP 1989
         6 Paul Edward ALBAUGH
         + Florence BAYLISS
         6 Betty Lee ALBAUGH b: 1928 d: 1980

        6   Margaret Kathryn ALBAUGH b: 19 FEB 1930
            d: 3 MAR 2001 m: 2 SEP 1949
        +   Hugh Harrison ORNDOFF
            b: 18 JUN 1920 d: 8 NOV 1984
            7   Ward Wise ORNDOFF
            7   Crystel Lynn ORNDOFF
            +   Seth KURTZBERG
                8   David Ward KURTZBERG
            7   Meridee Kay ORNDOFF
            +   Kirk Steven MUCCIARONE
                8   Anthony Edward MUCCIARONE
                8   Steven Ward MUCCIARONE
            7   Harrison Riley ORNDOFF b: 23 MAR 1957
                d: 14 DEC 1997
            7   Gordon Wayne ORNDOFF
            +   JoJo HALLER
                8   Gregory Wayne ORNDOFF
                8   Nickolas Riley ORNDOFF
                8   Crystal ORNDOFF
            7   Paul Edward ORNDOFF
            7   Lorena Calvert ORNDOFF
    5   Helen BODMER b: 14 AUG 1903 d: 20 MAR 1992
    +   Leonard GOSWELLEN
    5   John Perry BODMER b: 14 MAY 1905 d: 21 AUG 1977
    +   Eva
    5   Gordon BODMER
    +   Catherine
    5   Virginia BODMER b: 20 NOV 1909 d: 30 MAR 1980
    +   Paul MYERS
4   Richard Henry GOODE b:12 OCT 1875
    d: NOV 1925 m: 25 NOV 1894
+   Katherine C. S. DAVIS
4   Arthur Perry GOODE b: 27 APR 1877
    d: 21 APR 1949 m: 28 APR 1903
+   Susie Elizabeth COFFMAN b: 18 Oct 1880 d: 16 Oct 1973
4   Rosa L. GOODE b: 3 NOV 1880 m: 7 SEP 1901
+   Joseph L. HARTY
4   Blanche Catherine GOODE b: 23 MAY 1982
    d: 4 APR 1937 m: 10 SEP 1899
+   Clarence B. SEATON
    5   Edith Lillian SEATON b: 1/21/1901
    5   Welby Vincent Hackley SEATON b: 8/4/1902
    5   Olive Mildred SEATON b: 6/9/1904
    5   Gerald Ashby SEATON
    5   Anna Elizabeth SEATON

5 Sylvia Marie SEATON
5 Dorothy Lee SEATON
4 Walter Settle GOODE b: 8 OCT 1883
d: 15 AUG 1954 m: 13 JUL 1905
+ Alma LEMON
4 Annie Hamilton GOODE b: 30 SEP 1889 d: 11 OCT 1889
4 Ashby Peyton GOODE b: 9 JAN 1891 d: 1968
4 Clara May GOODE b: 26 JUL 1892 m: 5 NOV 1910
+ Frank T. VERMILLION
3 John B. GOODE b: 10/17/1857
+ Theresa GRUBB
3 Mary Jane GOODE d: died young, unmarried
**** 3 Edward Benjamin GOODE b: 17 DEC 1861 d: 1934
+ Eliza ELLISON b: 1860 d: 1935
4 Annie C. GOODE b: 1889
4 Mary GOODE b: 1890
4 William GOODE b: 1893 d: 1932
4 Nellie GOODE b: 1895
4 Randolph GOODE b: 1898
4 Robert GOODE b: 1899 d: 1959
2 Henry GOODE
+ Maria HIGGS
2 Benjamin GOODE
+ Elizabeth ANN
2 Catherine Roswell GOODE b: 3/28/1806
+ George SIMPSON
2 Clarissa GOODE
+ Hiram DAVIS of Va.
2 Harriet GOODE
+ William SWANN
2 Chloe GOODE

*Records for this generation from family Bible — Source Annie Goode Ish as listed in *Notes on Goode Family History* by Sister Teresa Clare and M.G.S. Chart 108, Seaton Lineage at Balch Library, Leesburg, VA.
**Records for this generation from family Bible owned by Hazel Harty Burns as listed in *Notes on Goode Family History* by Sister Teresa Clare and M.G S. Chart 108, Seaton Lineage at Balch Library, Leesburg, VA.
***Dates from gravemarkers at Middleburg Memorial Cemetery, Middleburg, VA
****From gravemarkers at Middleburg Memorial Cemetery, Middleburg, VA, and the 1900 U.S. Census. Census also shows Alice M(aude) Ellison living with the Goodes at the time.

Bodmer Family

DECENDANCY

*1 George BODMER b: 14 JUL 1831 Wuttenburg Germany d: 12 APR 1910
+ Margaret b: 1 DEC 1838 Germany d: 28 FEB 1912
   2   Mary BODMER b: 1857 not married
   2   Catherine BODMER b: 13 JAN 1859 d: 9 SEP 1922 not married
   2   George BODMER b: AUG 1864 not married
   2   John W. BODMER b: 30 AUG 1868 d: 2 FEB 1944
   +   Ella Lee GOODE b: 16 AUG 1874 d: 10 JUN 1952 m: 17 JAN 1901
      3   Margaret Goode BODMER b: 16 NOV 1901 d: 4 FEB 1986
      +   Paul Edward ALBAUGH
         4   Paul Edward ALBAUGH Jr. b: 26 DEC 1926
         +   Florence BAYLISS
         4   Betty Lee ALBAUGH b: 1928 d: 1980
         4   Margaret Kathryn ALBAUGH b: 19 FEB 1930 d: 3 MAR 2001
            m: 2 SEP 1949
         +   Hugh Harrison ORNDOFF b: 18 JUN 1920 d: 8 NOV 1984
           5   Ward Wise ORNDOFF
           5   Crystel Lynn ORNDOFF
           +   Seth KURTZBERG
              6   David Ward KURTZBERG
           5   Meridee Kay ORNDOFF
           +   Kirk Steven MUCCIARONE
              6   Anthony Edward MUCCIARONE
              6   Steven Ward MUCCIARONE
           5   Harrison Riley ORNDOFF b: 23 MAR 1957 d: 14 DEC 1997
           5   Gordon Wayne ORNDOFF
           +   JoJo HALLER
              6   Gregory Wayne ORNDOFF
              6   Nickolas Riley ORNDOFF
              6   Crystal ORNDOFF
           5   Paul Edward ORNDOFF
           5   Lorena Calvert ORNDOFF
      3   Helen BODMER b: 14 AUG 1903 d: 20 MAR 1992
      +   Leonard GOSWELLEN
      3   John Perry BODMER b: 14 MAY 1905 d: 21 AUG 1977
      +   Eva
      3   Gordon BODMER
      +   Catherine
      3   Virginia BODMER b: 20 NOV 1909 d: 30 MAR 1980
      +   Paul MYERS

2   Charles BODMER b: 16 APR 1871 d: 20 JUL 1894 not married
** 2   James F. BODMER b: 29 AUG 1873 d: 1947
  +   Alice W. BODMER b: FEB 1878 d:1959
      3   James BODMER b: SEP 1898
      3   Infant BODMER (not yet named at time of census) b: APR 1900
**2   Thomas BODMER b: 25 JAN 1876
***+1 Effie Mae HUTCHISON NOV 1880
      3   Pauline Hutchison BODMER b: 13 JUL 1905
      3   Louis Augusta BODMER b: 6 FEB 1906
      3   Evelyn Mae BODMER b: 29 NOV 1908
      3   Thomas Edward BODMER b: 1 FEB 1910
      3   Sue Virginia BODMER b: 18 JAN 1912
      3   William Page BODMER b: 25 MAY 1913
      3   George BODMER b: 1915
      3   Baby BODMER b: 1918
***+2 Henrietta MORAN after 1921
      3   Aurelia Botts BODMER
      3   Yona BODMER
      3   Gelston Paxton BODMER
** 2   Lewis H. BODMER b: 22 MAY 1878 d: 29 SEP 1905
** 2   Robert L. BODMER b: 25 APR 1881 not married

*Information from gravemarkers at Middleburg Memorial Cemetery and the 1900 Federal Census for Loudoun County.

**Birth dates from Loudoun County Virginia Birth Registers 1853–1879 and 1880–1896.

***Information from www.ancestry.com, Virginia Furrs, courtesy of Bill Furr.

Settle Family

SETTLE DESCENDANCY

*1 Henry SETTLE b: ABT 1785 Loudoun Co., VA;
  d: ABT 1845 Ohio m: ABT 1815
 + Margaret b: ABT 1790 d: after 1819
  2 Martin Luther SETTLE b: ABT 1819 Virginia
     d: after 1852 Loudoun Co., VA m: 29 MAR 1849
  + Julia DAVIS
     3 Margaret Clara SETTLE b: 28 MAY 1952; Loudoun Co., VA
        d: 13 SEP 1925 Aldie VA. buried Ketoctin Cemetery m: 22 JAN 1873
     + Samuel Perry GOODE b: 8 SEP 1852
        St. Mary's Co., Maryland d: 5 AUG 1893, Loudoun Co., VA
     ** 4 Ella Lee GOODE b: 16 AUG 1874
           d: 10 JUN 1952 m: 17 JAN 1901
        + John W. BODMER b: 30 AUG 1868 d: 2 FEB 1944
        ***5 Margaret BODMER b: 16 NOV 1901; d: 4 FEB 1986
           + Paul Edward ALBAUGH
              6 Paul Edward ALBAUGH Jr.
              + Florence BAYLISS
              6 Betty Lee ALBAUGH b: 1928 d: 1980
              6 Margaret Kathryn ALBAUGH
                 b: 19 FEB 1930 d: 3 MAR 2001; m: 2 SEP 1949
              + Hugh Harrison ORNDOFF
                 b: 18 JUN 1920 d: 8 NOV 1984
                 7 Ward Wise ORNDOFF
                 7 Crystel Lynn ORNDOFF
                 + Seth KURTZBERG
                    8 David KURTZBERG
                 7 Meridee Kay ORNDOFF
                 + Kirk Steven MUCCIARONE
                    8 Anthony Edward MUCCIARONE
                    8 Steven Ward MUCCIARONE
                 7 Harrison Riley ORNDOFF, 23 MAR 1957
                    d: 14 DEC 1997
                 7 Gordon Wayne ORNDOFF
                 + JoJo HALLER
                    8 Gregory Wayne ORNDOFF
                    8 Nickolas Riley ORNDOFF
                    8 Crystal ORNDOFF
                 7 Paul Edward ORNDOFF
                 7 Lorena Calvert ORNDOFF

        5 Helen BODMER b: 14 AUG 1903; d: 20 MAR 1992
        + Leonard GOSWELLEN
        5 John Perry BODMER b: 14 MAY 1905; d: 21 AUG 1977
        + Eva
        5 Gordon BODMER
        + Catherine
        5 Virginia BODMER b: 20 NOV 1909; d: 30 MAR 1980
        + Paul MYERS
    4 Richard Henry GOODE b:12 OCT 1875
       d: NOV 1925 m: 25 NOV 1894
    + Katherine C. S. DAVIS
    4 Arthur Perry GOODE b: 27 APR 1877
       d: 21 APR 1949 m: 28 APR 1903
    + Susie Elizabeth COFFMAN
    4 Rosa L. GOODE b: 3 NOV 1880; m: 7 SEP 1901
    + Joseph L. HARTY
    4 Blanche Catherine GOODE b: 23 MAY
       1982 d: 4 APR 1937 m: 10 SEP 1899
    + Clarence B. SEATON
    4 Walter Settle GOODE b: 8 OCT 1883
       d: 15 AUG 1954 m: 13 JUL 1905
    + Alma LEMON
    4 Annie Hamilton GOODE b: 30 SEP 1889; d: 11 OCT 1889
    4 Ashby Peyton GOODE b: 9 JAN 1891; d: 1968
    4 Clara May GOODE b: 26 JUL 1892; m: 5 NOV 1910
    + Frank T. VERMILLION

* First and second generation decendancy from from M.G.S. Chart 108, Seaton
Lineage at Balch Library, Leesburg, VA, and gravemarkers at Middleburg
Memorial Cemetery.

**Records for this generation from family Bible owned by Hazel Harty Burns
as listed in *Notes on Goode Family History* by Sister Teresa Clare and M.G.S.
Chart 108, Seaton Lineage at Balch Library, Leesburg, VA.

***Dates for fifth generation from gravemarkers at Middleburg Memorial
Cemetery, Middleburg, VA, and the 1900 Federal Census for Loudoun County.

Index of Names and Places

Meridee Orndoff Mucciarone is a 1976 graduate of Roanoke College in Salem, Virginia. She has worked many years in the publications field. Her interest in family and local history motivated her to compile this, her first book. She resides in Loudoun County, Virginia, with her husband Kirk, and sons Anthony and Steven.

www.ingramcontent.com/pod-product-compliance
Lightning Source LLC
Chambersburg PA
CBHW070224030726
47505CB00006B/1809